A MORGAN CALLED RED

Brooklands to Laguna Seca

Larry Ayers

ISBN 0-929758-20-X

Published by Beeman Jorgensen, Inc.
7510 Allisonville Road, Suite 120, Indianapolis, IN 46250 U.S.A.

Printed and bound in the United States of America
Cover design: Llew Kinst, Cupertino, California
Cover photography: The Laird Collection, Bob Dunsmore, Donna Dell'Ario

First Printing, November 1999

Contents

To the memory of my friend Vic Hyde
and to Morgan owners, enthusiasts, and racing drivers
in celebration of the 90th Anniversary of Morgans

Acknowledgements

Many thanks to the numerous individuals without whose contributions of material, time and patience this work could not have been accomplished: my partner and adviser, Donna Dell'Ario; Richard Laird, Dr. Jake Alderson and Dennis M. Rushton; my readers Bob Schmidt and Mark Bredt; Morgan Three Wheeler Club (MTWC) and its members – especially Stan Thorpe, Martyn Webb, Titch Allen, John Lindop, Bob Thredder, Dick Tuttle and Ray Olsen; The Brooklands Society archivist and librarian Tony Hutchings.

Friends in the MTWC helped greatly by providing missing components such as brake shoes, engine cams, literature and history. I am indebted to Gary Caroline, Chris Booth, Alan Goldsmith, Mike Sythes, Les Bolton, Bill Wallbank, Barry Davidson, Keith Lynsell, F.H. Douglass, Peter Morgan and others for their assistance.

Many of the photos in this book were provided from the Laird family collection. There are instances where photos have been obtained from scrapbooks and Morgan collections and it has been impossible to trace their source. Modern era photos were largely contributed by Vic Hyde, Donna Dell'Ario, Bob Dunsmore and the author. Additional thanks to those unnamed contributors and my apologies to anyone who I may have overlooked.

Foreword

I have never before had the honour of being asked to write the foreword to a book and I should normally be very hesitant about doing so were it not for two facts. First is the enjoyment I derived in the years 1933 to 1937 through being involved in a humble way with my brother, Henry Laird, in his enthusiasm for the Morgan "breed" in general and for "Red Johnnie" in particular. Second, in some ways even more remarkable, is the enthusiasm for "Red" by her present owner, Larry Ayers of San Francisco.

Henry Laird was named after his grandfather, Henry Hyndman Laird, who was one of the partners in the Birkenhead ship-building firm of Laird Brothers. Henry Hyndman was always said to have been the technical brain behind the design of the Laird-built ships of those days and I am happy to think that my brother Henry inherited this technical flair. Henry certainly had a great feeling for any piece of machinery and he had a real affection for his various "motors," which he regarded as having personalities of their own and which needed to be treated as individuals, if they were to give of their best. I do not think it fanciful to say that Morgans as a "breed" had just that personality, which appealed to Henry and which also clearly appeals to Larry Ayers, far away on the other side of the Atlantic Ocean and, indeed, on the other side of the North American continent. For this reason, I feel sure that Henry and his wife Barbara, who are no longer with us, must be happy to know that "Red" is in such good hands.

Richard Laird
Streatley-on-Thames, Berkshire, England, July 1997

Introduction

Morgan trikes were never highly prized vehicles. They were expendable and often junked after they crashed. They were small, easily broken up, and in the early days many were simply thrown on trash heaps, dumped behind hedges or left in fields to decay. During the World Wars when petrol rationing was in effect, many were stored and later ended up in junk yards. Out of a production of nearly 40,000 Morgan three wheelers from 1910-52 only about 2,000 have survived. A small number of these survivors have become racing trikes and occasionally appear on tracks around the world.

Morgans continue to be raced by enthusiastic amateurs while passengered and crewed by family and friends. These trikes appear like works in progress with engines swapped, ignition systems modified, gearboxes and sprockets altered and body panels reshaped.

In the 1930s, Morgans raced at such legendary tracks as Brooklands and Donington Park, competing against other light cars and motorcycles with sidecars. They raced on tracks, country roads and at hill climbs, breaking records and making history.

In 1961, a battered 1930 Morgan Super Aero was imported to the United States from England. Its owner disassembled it in an old shed in New England where it lay for six years. It was then sold to another three wheeler enthusiast who partially restored it in Michigan, owning it for ten years. During that time his research proved the trike had raced at Brooklands and at Donington Park in the 1930s, and in fact, held several world records. This Morgan was nicknamed, Red, by its racing driver, Henry Laird.

In 1977 I obtained Red, British registration YY 19, in a trade for two BSA three wheelers. Following extensive research and restoration, I raced it in 1984. It was subsequently sold and went back to England in 1990. In 1995 it was repurchased and returned it to the United States to again enter the racing arena.

This story about trike racing evolved out of 29 years of enthusiastic Morgan ownership of both three and four wheelers. During this time, I've collected photographs and literature, researched Morgan racing and explored the entire spectrum of Morgan ownership. This is the historical account of the racing Morgan called Red, the story of those who raced it and how it evolved to the present day.

Larry W. Ayers
San Francisco, 1999

Early History and Trials, 1930-34

Since 1910, many new Morgans had passed through the factory gates in Malvern Link. In late 1929 H.F.S. Morgan dispatched a particular 1930 Super Aero model to one of his dealers, Arthur Maskell, of "Maskell for Morgans." Maskell, aside from being a Morgan dealer, was also enthusiastic about racing. Instead of selling the Super Aero right away, he began using the trike in a slightly modified condition for several races, campaigning it at Brooklands. From day one his new 1930 Morgan became a racer. To increase its speed, he fitted a specially tuned 1926 ohv 50-degree JAP engine. He replaced the glass windscreens with sloping metal wind scallops on the cowl to decrease wind resistance. A grab handle device for his racing passenger was made by installing a hoop over the beetle back body work.

One of his races took place on August 16, 1930. Sponsored by The British Motor Cycle Racing Club, this BMCRC 10 lap three wheeler handicap race was open to members of the Light Car Club. Maskell beat Clive Lones in a close contest by averaging 53.32 mph. In 1932 Maskell ordered another personal Morgan, again a Super Aero, and sold the 1930 model to a student named John E.R. Palmer. Palmer ran the trike back and forth between his home and school, enjoying its speed and reliability.

Arthur *the rascal* Maskell, as he was sometimes called, had a friend by the name of Henry Laird, a grandson of the founder of the Cammell Laird shipbuilding firm in Belfast. Henry was another enthusiast who loved the sporty twin chain-driven Morgan vehicles and owned several over the years.

Henry named each of his various Morgans Johnnie, attaching a number. It was Henry's dad who first christened one of Henry's Morgans *Johnnie* having heard an old Music Hall tune titled *Johnnie Morgan Plays His Organ*; the name just stuck as a family joke that was easy to remember. Henry's first Morgan was a 1925 side valve JAP engined Aero, known as Johnnie I, with registration XX 7278, which he purchased in 1927. Johnnie II was another Aero with an ohv JAP dog-eared water cooled engine and registration RA 6559. *Dog-eared* related to the overhead rocker supports on the cylinder heads which resembled a dog's ears. This was replaced by Slug, a 350 ohv Sunbeam which was replaced by Johnnie III, CK 4187 in late 1929. Johnnie IV was a Super Aero with a later JAP ohv engine and cranked crosshead. The term crosshead referred to the two parallel horizontal chassis tubes at the front of the trike. The process of bending them upward, effectively lowered the chassis and center of gravity resulting in the cranked crosshead configuration. This was very advantageous for racing effectively lowering the chassis by two and one-half inches. He swapped Johnnie IV for a later 1931 Super Sports Johnnie V, also known as Johnnie Yellow until the name was shortened and simply became Yellow. It carried registration VN 2810. He owned another Aero which was a wide track with a straight tube chassis, i.e. the front horizontal chassis tubes were straight across without any bend in them. One F-model came into his ownership, RC 2399, which sported an 8 hp engine. Enthusiasm for motorcycles as well as cycle cars prompted ownership of a 350 side valve AJS and then a Henley with a sidecar.

Henry had been competing in trials with the Morgan he called Yellow, but he desired to race on the track as well, but didn't own a Morgan suitable for the purpose. He entered his trials Morgan at Donington Park on August Bank Holiday in 1932. Finishing in third place behind a Norton Sidecar, he realized that to be more competitive he needed a more suitable three wheeler.

A.C. Maskell driving Red at Brooklands on August 16, 1930 for a BMCRC race

Red at the Laird's home in Duffield, June 1933

An advertisement for the Zoller compressor featuring Red with a Zoller in place

Henry's wishes were answered when he contacted Arthur Maskell who remembered the Super Aero he had sold to John Palmer. Palmer was always strapped for cash and when approached by Maskell, agreed to sell the 1930 model to Henry Laird.

Henry named his new racer *Johnnie Red,* but soon dropped the prefix and called it *Red the Racer,* then just *Red*. It carried the registration YY 19. He registered it in the English Log Book at Pontings, Chadfield Road, Duffield, Derbyshire on May 15, 1933.

Red was a two speeder, meaning it had dual chains and sprockets on either side of the rear wheel for a final drive. The bevel box, just in front of the rear wheel, had two bevel gears and took its power from a prop shaft running through a torque tube to the clutch and flywheel attached to the engine. The engine was a 1096 cc (85 x 95 mm) V-twin JAP of 1926 vintage, water cooled, producing 40 bhp at 4200 rpm with a compression ratio of 5.4:1. It was one of the early *dog eared* models. With domed high compression pistons, this engine could possibly deliver 50 bhp depending on the carburetion, which equals about 90 mph on a lengthy straight. The trike made its racing debut at Brooklands while owned by Maskell and the engine was specially tuned for racing. Red was fast, but not as fast as it would become with its new owner, Henry Laird.

Henry was educated at Harrow. He was a very modest man, masking a determination to perform his best behind a desire for fun with a schoolboy shyness. In 1931, he joined the engineering firm of Michael A. McEvoy, Ltd. This firm, which had manufactured the McEvoy motorcycle, had been hit hard by the depression. McEvoy turned to the development of high speed cars which involved experimentation and use of superchargers. Henry loved going fast and soon became the firm's leading exponent for proving fast equipment. McEvoy later joined a venture with Laurence Pomeroy to manufacture and promote the German Zoller supercharger under license. These Zoller superchargers had been installed on a 6-cylinder Star, a SS1 Jaguar for Bill Lyons (the head of Jaguar), and a Val Page 650 cc Triumph vertical twin for racing at Brooklands.

The use of forced air into the induction system of engines was not new. On October 11, 1930, a Morgan with a 1098 cc Blackburne twin ran with a Sun-Villers blower at Brooklands. This two seater trike, driven by R.R. Jackson, finished third from scratch in the BMCRC Grand Cup and Championship meeting after achieving a speed of over 101 mph. This feat won him a Brooklands Gold Star. Another Morgan in the same race, driven by Clive Lones, achieved 100 mph, also winning a Gold Star. Clive also took home another award called the Wakefield Cup.

Henry Laird experimented with a Zoller installed on the JAP engine on Yellow, his trials car. Later, he transferred the setup to Red. Henry always used a chain drive on the compressor as belts in those days would slip and were not strong enough for the job. No blow off valve was used as a safety precaution should there be a backfire through the carburetor.

Racing blood seemed to course through Henry's veins and he thoroughly enjoyed trials work with Yellow. With Red, he could pursue road racing. His enthusiasm seemed infectious. When he proposed to Barbara Faraday, whom he married in 1929, Henry gave her the choice of either an engagement ring or a new Morgan. Barbara chose the latter and then became his stalwart passenger for trials. Henry who was 5'8" (a comfortable height for Morgan driving) had a brother, Richard Laird 5'6" tall, who worked in London and acted as his racing passenger whenever possible. Due to Auto Cycle Union (ACU) stipulations at locations such as Donington Park, women were still barred as passengers. The fact that women were not given wide acceptance in racing circles, however, did not keep Barbara from trying. On one occasion in 1934, she was wearing a crash helmet and leather jacket and was on the starting grid when spotted by Secretary Fred Craner, the race organizer. "Out you get," he ordered. "ACU regulations don't allow women passengers."

"How do you know I'm a woman?" retorted Barbara, confident of her disguise.

"Because of...." he made an expansive gesture, settling the matter. Fred Craner didn't have a lot of patience with people, and those who treated him with disrespect could become instant enemies, so Barbara complied. But, behind it all Fred had a kind heart, and was very efficient in what he did. Richard Laird again volunteered to passenger.

When not in the Morgan, Richard was often seen on his Brough Superior SS80 motorcycle. He remained a mainstay in many of the early races with Red.

Barbara, on the other hand, seemed more at home with Yellow, becoming quite proficient at bounding up on the tail of the trike to add traction at hill climbs. Her body weight served as ballast for trials. The sport of trialing (often called mud-plucking and similar to American off-highway vehicle use) consisted of going into the English countryside and navigating across meadows, up and down hills and through streams in order to challenge the terrain to its fullest. Barbara often emerged from trials and hill climbs completely covered in mud, and earned quite a reputation with the press as a real sportsman. Barbara enjoyed Red as well, especially during the many road tests which she and Henry entered.

Yellow was logically chosen over Red for trials work because its narrower body and higher chassis allowed increased clearance through passages and over rocks and road ruts. One of its early factory modifications consisted of changing the dropped chassis cross tubes for straight ones, narrowing the track and increasing ground clearance. This important modification permitted Yellow to get through tight spots and around and over obstacles during hill climbs where Red wouldn't stand a chance. Some of the places they squeezed through, like Hollinsclough in Derbyshire, were a challenge – even for a solo motorcycle.

Henry and Barbara on Litton Slack with Yellow during the MCC One Day Sporting Trial, October 17, 1931

In May, 1931, Barbara and Henry took Yellow to Wrotham Park near Barnet for the London-Edinburg Trial. A field of 62 cars and 9 sidecars had to climb Park Rash, one of the hills involved. Five Morgans, entered by John Hooper, Harry Jones, Kingdon, George Goodall, and Laird, had no difficulty with the incline, but only one of the sidecars succeeded. Hooper took a silver medal because of a restart on Tan Hill. The Lairds and the other Morgan men were each awarded gold medals.

Henry Laird gained valuable racing experience while participating with Yellow in the September 26, 1931, Seventh High Speed Reliability Trial at Brooklands in class K (cyclecars not exceeding 1100 cc). This was a meet sponsored by the Motor Cycling Club, Ltd. (MCC), founded in 1901. For this event, Henry ran against the Morgans of Arthur Maskell and H.J. Hooper. The Lairds didn't win an award but were pleased to see Maskell take home a gold. Yellow was destined to win a medal in the October 31, 1931, MCC Sporting Trial. In this event, a twin rear wheeled factory Morgan driven by Geoff Harris won a first class award. Laird and Swift, other Morgan competitors, each won silver medals.

Laird's Morgan was fitted with a lower windscreen which would not obstruct vision and this became a trademark for Yellow, making it easily recognized among the competitors. Most drivers of Morgans had to look over the windscreen anyway to see their way, the normal top of the glass falling about eye level.

The Lairds were very competitive and entered the London-Exeter Trial in late December, 1931. Geoff Harris and G.E. Swift were each out in twin rear wheeled Morgans. Other Morgan entries were Goodall, Clarke, Lowe, Hooper, Maskell, and Joe Turner. Laird bagged a gold medal as did Harris, Goodall, Clarke and Lowe. Joe Turner in his Blackburn Aero, snagged a silver. George Goodall from the Morgan Factory was in one of the new 60-degree JAP three speed Morgans.

Henry Laird became acquainted with a lot of Morgan enthusiasts through his trials and racing days. Friends like Clive Lones and T.A. (Tom) Rhodes joined him as team mates in the Relay Races at Brooklands. Rhodes, a competitive Morgan man, was born about 1903 and his family operated the well known garage of Portus and Rhodes in Liverpool. Tom's brothers, Sid and George, became expert motorcyclists.

Henry Laird was back at Brooklands on July 18, 1932 for the LCC Second Relay Race, but not in a Morgan. His mount was the 1 $^1/_2$ litre McEvoy special, a Wolseley Hornet which raced as the "C" car on McEvoy's team. His team mates drove an Austin and another McEvoy Special. They didn't finish among the top contenders.

The Morgan Factory entered another team with three trikes in the same race. Clive Lones was the "A," Tom Rhodes the "B" and Geoff Harris the "C" member. The Morgan Team carried a heavy handicap and were not started until nearly an hour following the lead team. Lones' trike was fitted with an oversized pressurized tank which carried 10 gallons of fuel. His trike was assembled after it left the Morgan Company as a load of bits and pieces. During his 30 lap allotment he was lapping at 94 mph and increased this to 98 before the motor's big end failed. Tom Rhodes took the token and quickly got up to speed, but had the misfortune of breaking a valve rocker. When Geoff Harris took over he drove for only 12 minutes before he had the same problem. There would be better days for the Morgan Team.

The first London-Scarborough Trial was introduced by the MCC on July 28, 1932. Laird entered Yellow, but broke a mudguard support near Retford in the early morning hours. He rousted a mechanic out of bed at a nearby garage. The bloke threw a mackintosh over his pajamas and accomplished an excellent welding job. Laird went on to win a Premier Award in the company of the other Morgan entries, Hooper, Hicks and Brand.

On September 3, 1932, Henry was listed in the MCC's program for the Eighth High Speed Reliability Trial at Brooklands. He was entered in the two lap handicap for passenger motorcycles and 3-wheeled cyclecars. His trike, one of six Morgan entries, competed against the Morgans of K.A. Twitchett, E.P. Huxham, A.L. Hicks, H.J. Hooper, and L.H. Creed. A Harley Davidson with a sidecar entered by R.W. Praill and a BSA with W.G. Cunninghame rounded out the field. Hooper took first, Twitchett second and Huxham placed third.

John Hooper was an interesting character and a very aggressive Morgan driver and competitor. He became interested in the sport of competing with motorcars at age 24 with an old Calcott car. When he entered it in the 1930 London-Exeter Trial, he caused quite a sensation by entering such an unlikely vehicle. Later, he decided this vehicle wasn't what he wanted for competitions and got into Morgans. He ordered an M-chassis Aero in black and it was registered as DH 8602. It served as his everyday transport as well as for trials. Through his trials work he met Henry Laird and became acquainted with Michael McEvoy, the expert tuner.

Henry and Barbara Laird entered Yellow in the 1933

Colmore Cup event. They were the only Morgan with a single rear wheel – three other Morgan entries were all using twin rear wheels. The Victory Cup Trial was next, but such a muddy mess that all the Lairds could do with Yellow was look up Red Marley Hill and wish for drier conditions. They buried the Morgan axle deep in the mud, but survived to come away with a third class award.

Yellow at the start of the Bemrose Trophy Race at Donington Park, March 11, 1933

The Lairds had a struggle with tire tubes and were always pulling out a valve stem or picking up sharp stones or other objects which deflated tires. Since Yellow had non-detachable wheels, the tires had to be pulled off the rims and the tubes either patched or replaced. Henry and Barbara developed a sixth sense in working together when changing tires and tubes on Yellow and through practice were able to get the time down to 12 minutes flat. These skills proved beneficial when, on March 11, 1933, the Lairds entered the East Midland Centre Bemrose Trial and won an award called the News of The World Cup. However, the Laird's luck wasn't destined to hold when they entered the Wye Valley Trial on April 8. On one of the rocky hills, Yellow punctured two tires, a front and the rear. But they pushed on and all three tires were flat by the finish. The experience Henry gained while campaigning Yellow would serve him well when he began racing Red, whose racing career was about to be resumed.

Yellow climbing with two punctured tires at the Wye Valley Trial, April 8, 1933

Until 1933, the only organized racing in England took place at Brooklands, which some people called *the concrete monster*. The track, located 21 miles southwest of London, between Weybridge and Byfleet, lies in Surrey. It was built at the personal expense of one man, the wealthy landowner Hugh Fortesque Locke King, and located on his unique country estate. Inspiration for its construction came at Briscia following the Targa Florio meeting while he was watching cars race from Germany, France and Italy. He saw great motorcars – fast motorcars – cars winning money. He came away with an awareness that the sport was spreading. England at the time allowed no racing on public roads.

Locke King took the opportunity to make racing in England a reality. He was a perfectionist and wanted to pursue his racing dreams through accomplishments on a grand scale. He transferred his ideas from paper into the hands of 2,000 Irish workmen who

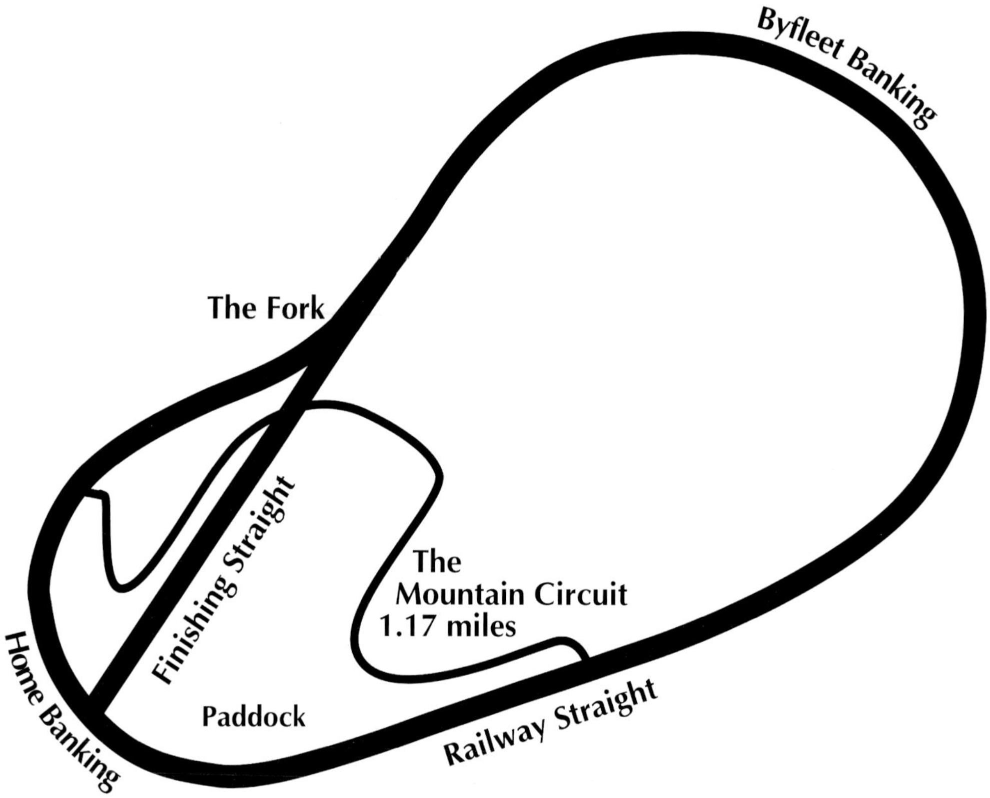

Brooklands 1909 - 1939
2.76 mile Outer Circuit

were hired to construct the track working in day and night shifts. The engineer for the job was H. Donaldson contracting through the firm of Price and Reeves. Work began in October of 1906 using reinforced concrete, a unique innovation at the time. It took 200,000 tons of gravel and cement, measuring 6 to 8 inches thick to lay the track surface. Seven miles of rail were laid on and around the course over which 6 locomotives hauled material for the bankings, arriving daily in 80 truck loads from London. The construction feat was an undertaking of immense proportions considering it was mostly done with picks, shovels, horses and carts, supported by 10 steam grabs and a steam navvy.

The project took 9 months to complete at a cost of around 150,000 Edwardian sovereigns, or the equivalent of about three million dollars by today's standards. The track, shaped like a huge pear-shaped concave bowl, was 100 feet wide and measured 2 miles, 1350 yards on the 50 foot line, or 2.76 miles on the Outer Circuit. Two steeply banked concave sections, known as the Byfleet and Home Banking rose to a height of 21 feet 10 inches and 21 feet 8 inches respectively. Brookland's designer had no idea what constituted a safe racing speed. More than one racer who didn't slow sufficiently when coming off the Finishing Straight approaching the main circuit flew over the top banking, usually with fatal results.

The course opened with a ceremonious luncheon in the Clubhouse on June 17, 1907. The guests then went on a tour of the new concrete track in their automobiles. Some larger machines sped around the track at nearly 80 mph. Track officials thought the layout was safe at speeds up to 120 mph. The opening meeting was held several weeks later on Saturday, July 6, 1907 with an attendance of around 13,500 spectators. The Brooklands Automobile Racing Club administered all racing at the new course. This organization, using its original initials, later became known as the British Automobile Racing Club, or the BARC.

The size of the track itself lessened the sensation of speed by about 20 mph. Viewing a Morgan trike at speed, it appeared like a flyspeck on your cocktail glass if you were on one side of the track trying to see the opposite side, even with field glasses.

A group of Americans visited Brooklands when the Indianapolis Motor Speedway track was getting underway. Although impressed by its grand scale, it doesn't appear that any of the British ideas went back to America. Britain, however, rightly laid claim to having the first hard surface engine speedway in the world! Furthermore, in the years from 1929 to 1936, the winning speed at the Brooklands 500 Mile Race was an average of about 4 mph faster than that achieved at Indianapolis. Finally, the land speed record was broken on no other closed circuit in history except at Brooklands.

A long way from being perfect, the track surface was so rough and bumpy that a pack of cigarettes in your pocket lost its tobacco content during a fast ride! The Big Bump at the end of the Member's Banking, caused by the Hennebique Bridge (designed by L.G. Mouchel) settling into the River Wey, appears legendary to anyone who has studied the track's history. It was given the name *Ermintrude*, and became famous for causing a car to fly 30 feet before landing. When racing over it, drivers would close the throttle or cut the magneto ignition to avoid blowing an engine.

Other aspects contributed to the discomfort at Brooklands – mostly the stench arising from the sewage farm on the perimeter and the River Wey, which ran through the infield and under the track in two places. But, despite the discomforts, this was the first British race track. It had no equal – no comparison. The drivers and their fast cars brought incredible color and atmosphere to the scene. The magic elixir of the fuel mixtures burned by the racing machines, and the scorched odor of Castrol R which lay above the surface in tiny wisps permeated one's nostrils, and fueled the dreams of racers and spectators alike.

Every type of vehicle ran at Brooklands. Bicycles, motorcycles and nearly every make of car and commercial vehicle were tested by various manufacturers, when the track wasn't being used for racing.

Brooklands also became famous for flying. With its aviation sheds, flying schools and runways, more than one pilot earned his wings while flying at Brooklands. On June 8, 1908, A.V. Roe made the first flight by a British pilot using his own aircraft. The distance flown was approximately 100 feet. In 1909, the flying grounds were first opened.

From its beginning, the track was a nuisance to some local residents. They claimed an invasion of privacy because of the constant noise from the unmuffled straight pipes used by a variety of machines. Legal battles were fought over the noise problem and in 1923, every racing vehicle using the track had to be equipped with a silencer or muffler called the Brooklands Can. This measure did reduce some of the complaints. It also reduced a car's performance. The restriction was imposed about the time of the opening of the Montlhèry Autodrome built near Paris in 1924 where no muffler regulation existed. More than a few drivers who were serious about record setting defected to the Continent. There they could race on the Montlhèry high speed banked 1.5 mile track which was linked to a road circuit for a total distance of 7.8 miles.

The first Morgan to race at Brooklands was owned by Harry Martin who participated in a BMCRC International Cyclecar Scratch Race on March 27, 1912. Martin's machine was a two seater fitted with a 986 cc JAP ohv twin engine. He trounced seven starters in this event, beating his nearest rival by 8 min and 32 sec at an average speed of 57 mph. His success so impressed the public that over 100 orders for new Morgans were forwarded to H.F.S. Morgan at the Morgan Motor Company.

In November of that year, H.F.S. Morgan also performed at Brooklands. He was successful in covering nearly 60 miles in one hour, coming up just several yards short. *The Cyclecar* stated: "In the motoring world, the hour record is regarded as one of the severest tests to which it is possible to subject a machine, be it car, motor bicycle or cyclecar. Few machines survive this test and those which do may be regarded as absolutely reliable and sturdily constructed vehicles." As a result of the success, Morgan Factory advertising literature soon carried this quote. "The Morgan is the fastest cyclecar in existence and it

July 25, 1931, the LCC Brooklands meet where the entries are dwarfed by the huge banking

proves by its wonderful performance at Brooklands that a three-wheeler not only holds the ground at any speed – but does so better than a four-wheeler."

The Cyclecar Club sprang up with an enthusiastic membership. Later their name changed to the Junior Car Club, reflecting the evolution of the cycle-car into the light motor car. This change was largely the result of racing at Brooklands.

The Brooklands track was closed from the outbreak of World War I in 1914 until 1920. From the early 1920s the track flourished with many Morgan drivers taking part in a variety of races. By the time Henry Laird arrived on the scene, Morgan racing at Brooklands was well established.

Before beginning any race, a driver had to learn the flag signals. The colors were blue, dark blue, black, green, yellow, and black and white checkered. The blue meant to keep low, someone is trying to pass. The dark blue meant caution, someone had crashed. The other flags, except for the black and white checkered, either meant slow or stop. The yellow meant to stop immediately.

A driver racing at Brooklands had to familiarize himself with the layout and what the track lines meant. Ten feet from the top of the banking there was a solid black line and it was dangerous to cross over it at speed. A dotted black line, 50 feet from the inner edge of the track was theoretically a 60 mph line, although a car lapping at 90 could be held on it. There was another black line at the turn onto the Home Banking. Slow cars were obliged to stay left of this as only very fast machines used the right side. At the Fork there were two other important lines which began at the end of the Byfleet Banking. A black line existed at the outer edge of the track, and another one was bright blue. If your speed was below 100 mph, you had to stay on the left side of the blue line. A caution was extended when coming out from behind the Member's Hill because under certain wind conditions the car could be blown up the banking. Drivers were further warned to be aware of the big bump encountered after leaving the Home Banking traveling toward the Railway Straight. As mentioned, ignitions had to be cut and throttles closed to avoid losing an engine when taking to the air at speed.

The Railway Straight was the fastest section of the track and measured half a mile long. It was so named because of the railroad tracks running on a parallel with it. The fastest one way speed ever timed over it was 151.97 mph achieved by John Cobb with his Napier Railton in 1935. Cobb later set the track's all time lap record at 143.44 mph on October 7, 1935 in the unlimited Class A category. A famous lady driver, Gwenda Stewart, also a Morgan enthusiast, set the Class E (under 2000 cc) outer circuit lap record with a speed of 135.95 mph on August 6, 1935 driving a Derby-Miller. In 1930, a new variation of the track called the *Mountain Circuit* or *The Mountain*, was born. It was the complete encircling of the Member's Hill measured 1.17 miles, and was formed by the Finishing Straight, Home Banking and the Fork driving in a clockwise direction. To get on it you turned right at the end of the Finishing Straight (which was something of a joke, as it was too short to fit its title effectively), traveled around the Member's Banking before reaching the Fork, then negotiated another right turn which brought you back to the Finishing Straight. Its shape resembled the letter D.

The first use of the *new circuit* was the Spring Meeting for the Junior Grand Prix. This race was won by Harold Purdy in a Bugatti. The BARC was soon staging races *Round The Mountain* and found them very popular with spectators, most of whom perched on the grassy slopes of the green island inside the circuit. The Mountain Championship was established as an annual BARC feature in 1931.

The last modification to the track was an infield road course comprising 2.26 miles, winding its way around both sides of the Finishing Straight and the River Wey, linking with the Outer Circuit. It was named the Campbell Circuit in honor of Malcolm Campbell for his land speed records and other racing accomplishments. Inaugurated in 1937, this section was entirely new concrete, the first laid since the track opened.

If a driver lapped Brooklands at over 120 miles per hour he received a special car badge. In 1921 one was awarded. After 1922, one was awarded for each year through 1927. The number then jumped amazingly until 1935 when 21 badges were awarded. Five women drivers were listed on the roster of 120 mph badge holders. Even more accomplished were the 17 drivers who lapped the circuit at over 130 mph with 5 women drivers in this elite group. On the other hand, if a driver lapped the outer circuit at over 100 miles per hour on a motorcycle, he was the recipient of a Brooklands Gold Star.

Early in the history of Brooklands, Mr. A.V. Ebblewhite, an RAC timekeeper, was instrumental in numbering car entries, getting drivers out of their brightly colored horse-racing smocks, and setting up the handicapping system. He tried a variety of handicapping methods. At first, cars started according to what they cost. This proved totally unworkable. By the fourth meeting at the track on September 14, 1907, he used a system starting the cars from different points, placing them so each driver could see the starter's

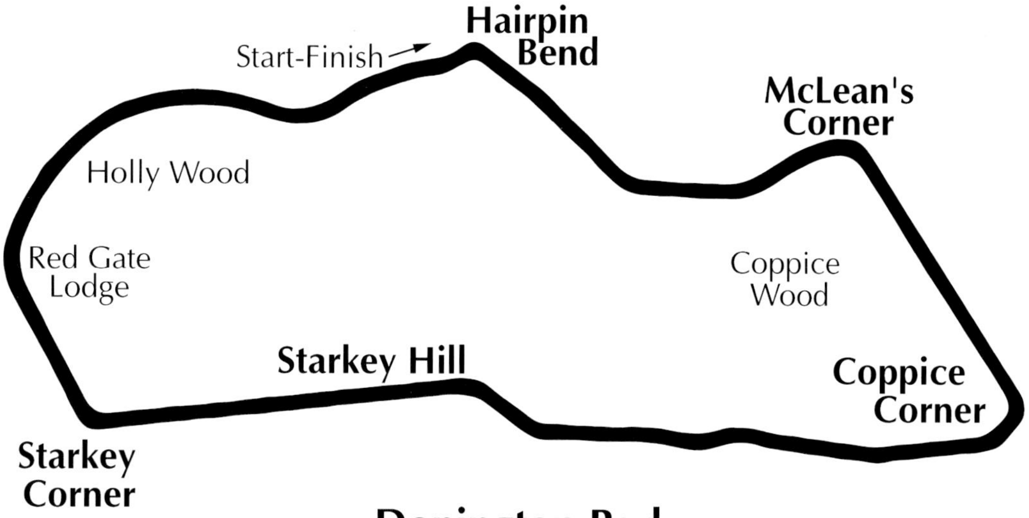

Donington Park
The first year's circuit - 2 miles 327 yards

flag – a tedious job. Finally, he initiated handicapping-by-time and this was adopted by June 1908. From then on *Ebby* became the official starter at Brooklands. This same gentleman kept and signed the timing sheet for Henry Laird during the Hutchinson 100 on October 10, 1936 when Henry won the Gold Star in Red.

Racing in the 1930s was an expensive proposition and not everyone could afford to do it. The average person earned 3 Pounds a week and a racing motorcycle cost around 75 Pounds. This was an era before people began trailering their machines to the track, and if any towing was done, it was usually by rope from the family vehicle. Henry Laird used a rope tow on several occasions to move Red. He used a Star automobile and a Sunbeam as towing vehicles, and even used Yellow in a pinch.

Henry's expenses were helped along by his good friend, Harry Lomas, who was a true *old time engineer* and opened shop in 1925. He was able to make anything out of a scrap of metal, whether forged, machined, or cast. When parts broke on either Red or Yellow, Harry made new ones – better than the originals. Without men like Lomas, who supported Morgans in competition, racing would have been more difficult, if not impossible, for many competitors. Harry, nicknamed *Rastas,* was given this unlikely title by his friend, George Patchet, who helped Rastas obtain his driver's license. Harry's son, Bill Lomas, won several world motorcycle championships including the Tourist Trophy and the 1956 Del Monda on a 350 cc Moto Guzzi.

Though organized racing in England was taking place only at Brooklands, there was a beautiful patch of land up in the Midlands where motorcycles had been having their meets since Whit Monday 1931. This location, called Donington Park, was owned by John Gillies.

Donington figured in history all the way back to King Canute when he founded the Langley Priory which owned the Donington Estate. Later, Thomas Plantagenet, the Earl of Lancaster, Leicester and Derby, purchased the land. There was a Castle Donington on the grounds at one time, but George, the Earl of Huntington, who purchased the grounds in 1594, knocked it down and built a mansion in its place. This became the main seat for the Earls of Huntington for many years.

In 1789, the Estate was bequeathed by Francis Hastings to his nephew, Francis, the Earl of Moira, who had been the General Governor of India. Francis built the present Donington Hall designed by W. Wilkins of Cambridge.

In 1933, the combined efforts of the Derby and District Motor Club and its Secretary, Fred Craner, resulted in a road course laid out in the park using existing drives and farm roads. The roads were widened to twenty feet and surfaced with tarmac. The completed circuit measured 2 miles 327 yards and wound through the hilly park accented with grassy slopes and tall trees.

In the early days of motorcycle racing at Donington, a

rider rode the distance from home to the track, removed the muffler, put in a hotter spark plug, changed the jet in the carburetor, and hopefully made it to the starting line for the first race. He did his best not to crash or fall off the bike during the day's events or he had no transport home. It was imperative for a machine to handle well, be very fast, and possess good braking.

Hand pushing a motorcycle, sidecar, or Morgan was the most widely used method of starting for most motorcycle races. A battery and starter motor only added unwanted dead weight to the racing profile. There was already a weight handicap in the Morgan or sidecar when the vehicle had to carry a full sized passenger.

Riders needed concentration to pull everything together as the Donington track was very fast. The circuit demanded a variety of driving skills with its high speed bends, a bottom gear right angle corner, a second gear section, a funnel through the woods allowing high speed through the gateway, and a climbing right hander.

Moving away from the start, the course ran uphill for about 150 yards, then made a turn of 45 degrees to the right, rising sharply to Hairpin Corner. This wasn't banked on the inside, and when taken too fast, could bring on some anxious moments. After crossing a bridge, the course wound through Coppice Woods with a right hand bend at McLeans Corner. Then it rose a quarter mile to Coppice Corner, another right hand bend. For about the next thirty yards, it passed farm buildings in a narrow no passing zone. A half mile straight followed, then a right-left S-bend, and another straight up Starkey Hill leading to Starkey Corner. Coming off the straight into Starkey Corner also pumped adrenaline for rookies. A driver needed to brake adequately since the corner had no walls and there was no way to gauge the curvature. After the right corner, another short straight came to Red Gate Lodge and on to Holly Wood with a gradual right curve, leading into a downhill winder which ended back at the start-finish line.

Donington Park, located about 6 miles southeast of the center of Derby and 12 miles southwest of Nottingham, became England's premier road racing circuit, the first licensed race track in England. Shortly after its first official race on March 25, 1933, it became a household name.

The Lairds' home was only about 15 miles from the Donington Park track, and Henry was destined to visit that location for some serious motoring competition.

Due to printing and advertising problems, the first meet at Donington was not very well attended. Classes were run for races with 850, 1100 and 1500 cc machines, both supercharged and running aspirated, i.e. with carburetors only. This track meet was mentioned in the press and word got around by the second meet. But at this meet, over half of the 51 cars entered failed to start. The large crowds that day, numbering between 9 and 10 thousand, still enjoyed their picnics in the beautiful surroundings of the park. As the first racing season ended, things were beginning to improve.

Henry Laird's first race with Red took place at Donington Park on April 17, 1933 in the Passenger Machine Event. His brother, Richard, passengered. The JAP engine ran with Lodge H1 plugs and a 50/50 fuel mixture through an Amal carburetor with a 220 main jet. The compression ratio (c.r.) was 8.7:1 on this very hot day. Off to a great start, they were leading the field by 100 yards at the end of lap one when the magneto timing slipped. This thrilling start whetted the Lairds appetite for more action.

For the LCC Relay Races at Brooklands on July 22, 1933, the Morgan Factory freshened up the paint on their Team No. 5 entry by re-spraying the trikes in scarlet with silver wheels. With double disc Andre Hartford shock absorbers fitted to a hoop over the rear wheel on Laird's Red, and on Rhodes' car, an oval hole was cut in the top of both beetle backs steel body work to allow for clearance. Strong steel cage work was welded on top of the oval opening and a canvas cover fitted over this.

Tommy Rhodes' JAP Morgan was the "A" entry, Henry Laird's, Red, the "B" entry, and H.C. Lones' JAP Morgan, the "C" entry. George Goodall managed the team while H.F.S. Morgan stuck to the business end of things, taking no active part in running the team, trusting the track decisions to George. Each team car was designated to run 30 laps to complete the total distance of 250 miles. If one car failed to make the 30 laps, the next car could make up the balance, but also had to do its own 30 laps. When a driver had completed his laps he handed a sash to the next team driver. Individual handicapping was used with the "C" car being the fastest, but if the "C" entry had trouble in practice, the team couldn't start. Once a car finished its turn, it couldn't go back on the track if one of the other cars failed. Cars of up to 1 1/2 liters were permitted. Twenty-seven teams started the race.

Henry set up Red with KLG plugs, sparked by an ML magneto, burning RD1 fuel. The Amal ran a 760 jet with a 9.8:1 c.r. and the engine was using Castrol R. Richard Laird was along to passenger.

During practice the Morgan team attempted radio contact by using loudspeakers in the cars. The track noise, however, defeated the purpose. The experiment attracted the news media and their newsreel cameras. The news crews faked a filming of the use of the speaker system in their attempt to explain how it should work, but all this did was subtract from the time needed to properly prepare the cars for the race. The Morgan Team had an additional problem when crossing the black line during practice but didn't explain this to the officials at the time. They were reprimanded on race day.

Rhodes, in the "A" car, got off to a great start, and was soon reaching lap speeds around 100 mph, taking one lap at 102 mph. This was the first time either a cyclecar or three wheeler had reached this speed, but it didn't last. Experiencing engine trouble, Rhodes came in and handed the sash to Laird. Starting with a cold engine, Laird soon reached speeds of 90 mph and attained one lap of 99.8. After 10 laps, bumpy Brooklands bit the Morgan and a tie rod broke shortly after Henry was cautioned for trespassing over a forbidden line when crossing the Fork. Was this Brooklands' revenge for violating a race rule? This left Lones with a lot more than his own 30 laps to cover. His little 731 cc JAP was soon reaching 95 mph and he had tied up third place by the seventieth lap. Twenty laps remained. Goodacre's supercharged Austin 7

The LCC Relay Race at Brooklands on July 22, 1933. Red is on the front row nearest the camera

The Morgan factory team entry for the Brooklands 1933 LCC Relay Race. Left to right: Tom Rhodes, Henry Laird, Richard Laird and Clive Lones

1933 Brooklands LCC Relay Races – George Goodall, the Morgan factory *works* manager and the team manager for the races helps push start Red

Pushing off at the start of the August 7, 1933 Donington Park Bank Holiday meet. Laird, in Red, number 91 at right, just in front of Rhodes; Hooper's Aero on the far left

Morgan trike. They averaged 82.99 mph. Hooper was quite pleased that he was nearly as fast lapping the track as the Morgans from the Factory Team.

Henry and Richard Laird went to Donington Park on August 7, 1933 for the Bank Holiday Monday meeting. Suffering with two taped broken ribs, Henry was in some discomfort. On July 17 as he returned home from a shopping trip in Yellow, he overturned while avoiding an oncoming bus and an overtaking car. He was summoned for a hearing at the Belper Police Court when it was alleged that he drove without due care, but the case was dismissed. Henry later admitted to friends that he was driving too fast for the conditions.

Bank Holiday at Donington – Richard, Barbara seated on Red and Henry Laird. Hooper's Aero is in the foreground. Note the passenger grab handles on both trikes.

Red was running the 1096 cc water cooled JAP and was burning a 50/50 petrol/benzole fuel mixture metered through the Amal with a 220 jet. An ML magneto fired the Bosch plugs with a c.r. of 8.3:1 and gear ratios of 6.25 and 4.5:1.

In the final race of the day, Laird's main competition was from H. Tozer on a 596 Norton and W.E. Bury on his 750 Douglas. Other riders were Collett, who quickly moved out in lap one, but was edged out in lap two by Tozer with Laird trying to get past D.J. Allard on his Brough Superior. Laird was being chased by Bury. The fifth lap saw J.L. Duke on an Aerial try to pass a Morgan while coming into the hairpin. He locked up everything and overturned, receiving serious injuries. Richard and Henry managed to finish in second place behind Tozer with an average speed of 54 mph for a lapsed time of 24 min 23 seconds. John Hooper was also in the field, along with Tom Rhodes and his new 994 cc JTOR engine. Neither of these Morgan drivers had any success this day.

September 9, 1933, brought a return trip for the Lairds to Weybridge and the Brooklands track. The

was close behind, but Rhodes pushed on, moving ahead of Tuson's Fiat after 10 more laps and into second place. He managed to hold this to the end, giving the Morgan Team a well earned second place with an average speed of 89.01 mph.

When the handicaps were factored, the Alan Hess' team of stripped MG Magnas, with Charlie Martin, G.W.J. Wright and Hess took first with an average of 88.62 mph. The team with Tuson's Fiat 8 and Robins' and Levy's MGs took third averaging 73 mph. The works Austins held their lap speeds at an average of 91.60 mph with Driscoll, Barnes, and Goodacre to place fourth. In fifth was the McEvoy team with the McEvoy Special, Greaves' Frazer Nash, and Hooper's event was the M.C.C. High Speed Trial and the entire meeting ran from 11 AM until 7:30 PM, possibly setting a record for any Brooklands meeting.

In the two lap passenger handicap, Maskell, with a 4 second handicap, was beaten by Hicks, carrying a handicap of 30 seconds and finishing at 79.94 mph. George Brough finished in third running at scratch.

The one hour high speed trial was the next event on the program and featured 39 starters. First Class Awards were presented in class K to Laird for 69.05 mph and to H.J. Hooper for 79.74 mph. Jefferies gained a silver at 60.69 mph, and Hicks, a bronze for his 52.59 mph finish.

Maskell lost his low gear chain. Actually, an official found the chain on the track and Maskell didn't know he had lost it until he tried to restart after experiencing engine trouble. His trike didn't run well after that and he finally called it a day after 8 laps.

Joe Huxham, while not running in the High Speed Trial, was persuaded by Laird to run in one of the Relay Races for three laps. Right at the start he blew up his engine! Later, following the meet, Laird, feeling somewhat responsible, entertained him at the Hand and Spear Hotel near Brooklands. They developed a lifelong friendship.

The Brookland's Relay Race for three laps was won by Laird's *Red* Team comprised of Red, Hooper's Aero, and Rodney Bainbridge on his Rudge machine posting a team speed of 72.18 mph. Behind them was the team of W.J. Jenness' Rudge, H. Jones' Cotton, and G.M. Bryant on his Velocette.

George Brough brought out a new machine, his very striking SS 100 and banking sidecar. The machine represented the new 1934 *100s* which featured dual magnetos and carburetors, and a special pressurized lubricating system serving the big end, timing gear, and pistons. A four speed foot-operated gearbox and fully enclosed chain were featured. It appeared very compact and sported a 2 1/2" shorter wheel base than previous models. Had it not been for a slipping clutch, the new machine might have captured the Premier Award. Nevertheless, it made a good impression on the spectators and the press.

George Brough became a close friend of the Lairds, introducing them to a pub called Shardlow near Donington Park where they used to retire for refreshment following a race. The pub was located on a sharp left-hand bend just beyond a humpbacked bridge. All of them used to park their vehicles in front of the pub and had several near misses as traffic came whizzing around that blind left-hand bend.

Richard Laird recalled how George Brough used to keep an eye on him when he had a bit too much to drink referring to him as "Rough Exterior" which sort of rhymes with his motorcycle, Brough Superior. Richard was never sure of the reference, but surmises that George may have been more concerned for the welfare of the motorcycle following a pub visit than for Richard's own personal welfare.

Llandrindod Wells was the next setting for the International Six Days' Trial (ISDT) and four Morgans entered under British Club teams. Geoff Harris brought out the dual rear wheel three speeder, WP 2928. Another two speeder dual rear wheeler was driven by Cole. Goodall was piloting his MX2. Henry and Barbara Laird were campaigning in Yellow but didn't get far as they sheared a center pin on the second day. Harris and Goodall had their share of problems, but went on to attain gold medals.

Henry Laird borrowed the factory's twin rear wheel three speeder WP 2928 in November for the ACU Team Trial and represented the East Midlands Center. Against the solo machines of Len Heath, Holdsworth and the Morris' Baughan-Python sidecar with sidecar wheel drive, the Laird's team came in last after losing 312.5 marks.

Outside the Hand & Spear Hotel during the September 1933 Brooklands MCC meet. Left to right: Hooper's Aero, Red, Yellow, Bainbridge's Aero and his Rudge motorcycle

Donington Park
Circuit from 1934 to late 1937 - 2 miles 971 yards

During the season, because of his excellent performances, Henry Laird earned a place in the British Expert's Trial. The BSA three wheeler driver, G.A. Norchi, was also in this class with his front wheel drive trike. Both entered the event, but had their entries refused. After much discussion over the controversy, Laird complained in the press and a reply was printed in the November 11, 1933 *Motor Cycling* magazine. It discussed the fact that while three tri-car drivers had won several awards in open trials, their inclusion in this event was impossible on certain grounds. "First, The Palmer Challenge Trophy was presented to the club for, and inscribed as, 'For the best sidecar performance.' Second, Several hills are quite unsuitable for tri-cars. Third, There is a regulation stating that 'Drive must be transmitted through one wheel only'." This immediately ruled out Norchi's fwd BSA and Harris' twin rear tired Morgan. It was decided, therefore, to invite Laird, Harris, and Norchi to enter on sidecar machines, knowing that at least one of these sportsmen had experience with sidecars. "In conclusion, surely it is not necessary for Mr. Laird to buy a motorcycle and sidecar for the British Expert's Trial," noted R.G.J. Watson, the Organizing Secretary.

Henry wrote to the press asking why he should compete all season with a Morgan, and then change to a sidecar for one event. He stated, "Surely this is an open admission of the Morgan's superiority when competing against motorcycles and sidecars."

The London-Exeter Trial saw Laird, Goodall, Huxham, Campbell, and Kelleher win silver awards. But the Yellow Morgan didn't distinguish itself enough to receive a Premier Award. Other Morgan entrants, Aldington and Euston, each received bronzes.

Morgans competed against motorcycles at the Colmore Cup Trial, although this year twin rear wheels were not allowed. Henry and Barbara entered Yellow. In spite of the lack of a run up on many of the hills, they completed the course with a loss of only 57 marks. This gave them the Bayliss Cup for the best three wheeler.

On April 2, 1934, motorcycle racing started a new season at Donington Park on a revamped circuit featuring a mile straight between Starkey Hill and Coppice Corner. Track modifications straightened out the S-bend at Starkey Hill. This straight stretch now ran for an additional 300 yards to the new Starkey Corner where drivers had to make a sharp right hairpin back to a parallel run toward Red Gate Corner. A sharp left returned to the old course near Red Gate Lodge. The distance from Coppice Corner to Starkey's Corner was now nearly a mile enabling acceleration to speeds of 100 mph.

Henry and Richard Laird entered Red in the 1100 cc event for sidecars and three wheelers on this very cold Easter Monday. The 1096 cc water cooled JAP was breathing 50/50 fuel through an Amal with a 220 jet. The Bosch plugs were fired by an ML magneto and the c.r. was 8.25:1. Sprocket ratios were 6.25 and 4.5:1. The usual battle was with Kim Collett's Norton. There were 10 entries in the race for sidecars and three wheelers, but only 7 actually started. This time Red surged ahead on the third lap, taking victory from his rival, Kim Collett. At 55 mph in a time of 27 min and 59.8 sec, Laird set a new 10 lap record for sidecars and three wheelers. There were only three drivers left at race end and Kim's 596 Norton placed second at 53.7 mph. W.H. Rose's 596 Norton took third at 52.9 mph.

Henry Laird next made an appearance at Donington driving a 1454 cc McEvoy Hornet. In the fourth race he was entered in the class for un-supercharged machines up to 1500 cc. A contest developed with S.G. Casswell driving a Frazer Nash, and T.A.W. Thorpe also in a Frazer Nash. Laird led the first lap with the others in close pursuit. On the fourth lap, Casswell managed to squeeze past into first, but then made an error at Starkey's Corner sliding into the grass, spinning around twice, allowing both Laird and Thorpe to get past. Henry Laird finished first in 13 min 23.8 sec at 57.5 mph. His fastest lap was 2 min 38 sec at 58.32 mph. He was very pleased with his performance on the track during this showery overcast day.

The Mercury Trophy won by Henry Laird at Donington in 1934. The inscription reads, "D. & D.M.C. Donington Park Road Races, H. Laird 1934." Height is 6 3/4" overall.

Red was back at Donington Park on May 20, 1934 for the Whitsun meet sponsored by the Derby and District Motor Club. Some 20,000 spectators turned out for the days' events. Henry had Red set up with the big 1096 cc JAP running Lodge H1 plugs and breathing through an Amal with a 220 jet. His passenger, Richard, was ready for the 10 Lap Race for unlimited cc for sidecars and three wheelers. This was one of the most exciting events of the day, with a closely fought battle between W.E. Bury on his 750 cc Douglas sidecar and Laird's Morgan. Red experienced ignition misfiring on the 1st, 2nd and 10th laps and this resulted in being beaten by the Douglas machine by a close margin of three seconds. Red's second place finish was with an average of 55.42 mph in 27 min and 48 seconds. H. Tozer, on a 490 Norton, finished in third with a speed of 54.22 mph. These performances were good, but didn't break the existing 10 lap record for the new circuit of 2 miles 1000 yards at Donington for sidecars and three wheelers set by Laird in April. With the number of turns, Red must have been very quick on the straights.

The 1934 Morgan factory sponsored team with their support at Brooklands. Left to right: Clive Lones, H.F.S Morgan in dark suit, Henry and Richard Laird, George Goodall (wearing tie) and Tom Rhodes

The Relay Race for 1934 at Brooklands took place on July 21st. The Light Car Club's annual classic had 18 teams competing. The Morgan team, Number 4, featured Tommy Rhodes' 998 cc JAP as the "A," Laird's Red with a 998 cc JAP as the "B" and H.C. Lones as the "C" with his 730 cc JAP engine. Red was set up with 14 mm Lodge plugs firing Shell N4 fuel and using Castrol R oil. The engine ran an ML magneto and an Amal carburetor with a 720 jet. Richard Laird was passengering.

The distance was 90 laps or about 250 miles. Each team member did as expected and carried his share of the 30 laps. H.F.S. Morgan was there cheering on his team with Mr. G.H. Goodall lending support. The Morgan team ran the fastest actual time despite a heavy downpour during the last hour of the race. Lones' efforts placed the Morgan team in sixth place despite the wet track. When the eighteenth lap was spent, he was running in third position. He moved up to second when the Fiat, driven by Tuson, broke a connecting rod. With their heavy handicap the Morgan Team managed an average speed of 90.91 mph. This put them in second place again, the same as the previous year. However, the previous year, the team was involved in some controversy over crossing the black line and the press thought this kept them out of the winner's circle in 1933.

The Austin team was victorious by 5 minutes, but that did little to dampen the spirit of the Morgan Team and their many supporters. Afterward, their celebration at the Ship Hotel in Weybridge was attended by Joe Huxham, a Morgan enthusiast in his own right and a finisher in 9th place with the West Hants team. Charlie Curtis, also known affectionately as *Fatty* Curtis, joined the Morgan team in the amiable consumption of several pints of bitter.

Donington again provided the venue for the August 6 Bank Holiday meeting. Red was sporting the 1096 cc water cooled JAP fired with Champion R11 plugs and 50/50 fuel mixture through a track type Amal with a 250 jet of Laird's own fabrication. The ML magneto provided the spark to the cylinders with an 8.25:1 ratio. Richard Laird was again passengering. The engine acted up during practice, so they changed the magneto and experimented with Lodge H1 and R1 plugs. The magneto misfiring continued, and later, both magnetos were found to be faulty. This race left the Lairds unplaced and provided another lesson in race preparation.

The International Six Days' Trial took place in Bavaria, Germany in August. Henry and Barbara entered Yellow and were in the company of Geoff Harris' new car from the factory, an MX2 Sports with straight cross tubes and a 16-inch rear tire on a special rim. Harris ran well until the final speed test when the engine broke an inlet valve rocker. He carried on, running on one cylinder to finish the course. R.C. Mead, another Morgan entry, couldn't get up Ettaler Strausse on the third day and retired. Henry and Barbara, on the other hand, had no trouble with the Ettalberg Mountain and went on to capture a gold medal with Yellow.

The McEvoy Special was pressed into service for August 18, 1934 at Donington. Henry Laird was entered in the 25 mile handicap along with 12 other cars. The 1454 cc engine was running Champion R11 plugs, ignited by a Scintilla magneto. Two B type 20 mm Rag carburetors with 64 mains and 98 power jets

On the banking at Brooklands during the 1934 Relay Races. Left to right: R.B. Watson, J.D. Barnes, W.J.B. Richards and Laird up near the top. Because of the handicapping, Morgans began near the end.

metered the 50/50 fuel mixture. The compression ratio was set at 8.9:1 and the differential had a ratio of 4.3:1.

Yellow at the ISDT, August 27, 1934

It was a very hot day and Henry got off to a good start running against T.C. Harrison's Ford and a Singer driven by E. Hodges. The McEvoy got out in front for three laps before the plugs oiled up and the car retired. After that, the Ford stayed in front for a time but others in the pack were gaining fast. Cyril Paul in a Riley and Charles Martin in his Bugatti had started on the 15 second mark. Another Bugatti driven by C.S. Staniland, had started at scratch and was picking up seconds on every lap. The Midget of Dunfee had an entire credit lap as well as a 60 second start and was still a threat. On each lap the cars seemed to get faster and faster. One lap by Staniland was recorded at 69.51 mph, a new record for the course. Lindsay Eccles held the record previously at 69 mph.

The excitement mounted as the race progressed and the crowd was standing as the cars roared down the hill past the paddock. On the 5th lap the Ford and Richardson's Riley were still in front, but stood no chance of winning. Paul's Riley was still leading the two Bugattis, but not for long. On the next lap, Staniland's Bugatti caught that of Martin and the Riley of Richardson fell back. The following lap saw the Staniland Bugatti on the bumper of Paul's Riley and the crowd was listening for the engine's sound at the top of the hill. As the cars sped under the bridge, the Bugatti ducked by the Riley to the satisfying roar of the crowd. Two laps later he was still in the lead as the checkered was waved and the crowd responded with a great cheer. Following the race it was determined that Staniland's Bugatti had broken the record for 10 laps with a speed of 68.79 mph taking the record from Lindsay Eccles at 66.99 mph.

The 10 lap, 25 mile handicap results for cars up to 3 liters were: 1st - C.S. Staniland (2.3 litre Bugatti S, running scratch) 22 min 23.6 sec - 66.792 mph. 2nd - Cyril Paul (1,808 cc Riley, 15 sec start) 22 min 53 sec - 67.30 mph. 3rd - C.E.C. Martin (2.3 litre Bugatti S, 5 sec start) 22 min 56 sec - 67.194 mph. Henry could only watch and wish he'd been able to compete.

An interesting article appeared in the September 14, 1934 issue of *Light Car* from the Manager of the Morgan Factory promoting the new F-Model. "It's the four cylinder that carries a full four-passenger compliment at an annual tax of four Pounds Sterling. Its initial price and annual running costs are less than half what you'd expect to pay for a four wheeler of equal performance. Speed up to 70 mph and petrol consumption of 40-45 mpg, coupled brakes, independent wheel springing, three speeds and reverse. Twelve months' sport car performance at the cost of six. It is smart and comfortable, is low sprung and holds the road like a leech."

The London-Exeter Trial on December 28, 1934 had several Morgan entries, including Laird, this time driving an F-model Morgan. It was fitted with a Zoller supercharger, chain driven. This was undoubtedly the result of McEvoy's becoming an agent for the Zoller. Other Morgan entries in this event were D.C. Campbell with an MX4 barrel back SS and K.P. Roberts in a JAP Super Sports. The Morgan factory was represented by Jim and George Goodall and Harry Jones. While passing through town on the way to the event, they somehow managed to collide with each other, resulting in considerable damage to Goodall's trike and less to Jones' trike, a Matchless Sports with 3 speeds and twin rear wheels.

Starting at Virginia Water, Laird was unsuccessful on Fingle Bridge due to excessive wheelspin. Jones and Jim Goodall managed Fingle Bridge all right, but then Goodall crashed into a stone wall and was finished. Harry Jones went on to Simms Hill, but failed here, and slid backwards. He did however, maintain the distinction of being the only factory representative to finish the course.

Racing For Records, 1935-37

Red with Zoller supercharger mounted on the JAP 996 JTOR engine. The left front tire wear courtesy Brooklands

When Henry entered the Colmore trial in February of 1935 with Yellow he installed a type 4 Zoller supercharger. Two large alloy plates mounted over the lower left chassis tube held the Zoller in place at the bottom. Another mounting plate connected the rear of the Zoller to the top chassis cross tube. It was chain driven by the engine's flywheel. A long induction tube carried a boost pressure of 12 pounds into the engine. Despite the supercharger, this was one of the rare times when the Lairds finished a race but failed to win an award. The organizers had insisted on the use of standard instead of competition tires.

The debate of whether or not the use of competition tires should be permitted in trails work revolved around the special tires used by trade entries at motorsport events. Several motorcycle publications aired the feelings of George H. Goodall from the Morgan Factory. He thought specialized machines using competition tires at certain trials should be severely handicapped. He favored standard tires to equalize the competition, arguing there would be more entries at trials events if ordinary competitors felt they had a chance against the trade competitor's greater advantage with competition tires.

Henry Laird, who enjoyed writing letters and articles, disagreed. His position was that certain machines were fitted with competition tires as standard equipment. It would be ludicrous if the man buying such a machine had to buy two standard tires before he could run in a reliability trial. "Let the Motor Cycling Club have its way as far as cars are concerned," he said, "but, should they decide to cater entirely for cars, why not drop the name of 'Motor Cycling Club' and rename it 'The Club for Cars Only?' Going to a trial with standard tyres rather reminds one of a rider riding in a trial in a dinner jacket." Henry also felt that, in his experience, tires were far from being one of the big expenses in a trials season. Entry fees and incidental expenses were the greatest costs.

Richard Laird also got in his two cents worth. He went to print stating that it was a fallacy to say that it is more costly to buy competition tires, which will probably last the year, than to buy new standard tires for every trial. "One might, indeed, as well ask two cup tie teams to play without studs in their boots on the grounds that they would give a worse, if more amusing, exhibition of football."

Something special took place when the Lairds entered the April 22, 1935 race at Donington. Henry transferred the Zoller from Yellow to Red and used it for the first time on his racer. McEvoy was present to offer advice during the 10 Lap Passenger Race for Three Wheelers and Motorcycle Combinations.

Cyril Hale, known as Charlie, was also entered for his first race in a new Morgan, a MX4 twin carbed, barrel back Super Sports. His enthusiasm had been building

Henry and Richard Laird during a relaxed moment with Red at Donington, May 18, 1935

Action at Donington Park on May 18, 1935 for the Grand Prix 10 mile Passenger Machine Race. Left to right: Kim Collett/596 Norton, W.E. Bury/746 Douglas, H. Tozer/596 Norton with Laird at the back with Red fitted with 1096 JAP and Zoller compressor

since spectating at a race featuring Morgans at Donington the previous year. He felt that a specially prepared Matchless could compete with the big JAP engines. However, while the Matchless was a smoother running engine, it lacked the brute horsepower and torque possessed by the JAPs.

Another entry, John Hooper, proved to himself that his ex-Jackson racer was more suited for wide-open throttle racing at Brooklands than campaigning at Donington. This special had minimal brakes, the wrong chassis set up for a twisty circuit, and plugs which kept oiling. After borrowing some plugs from McEvoy in Laird's pit area, Hooper began running better, but flipped the Morgan before Star key's Corner when a solo motorcycle cut him off. He landed on three wheels after turning a complete somersault! His passenger was shaken up a lot and the Morgan had broken a chassis stay. Repairing it with wire, he borrowed a passenger, one of Laird's friends, and competed in the afternoon race.

Cyril Hale gave it his best shot as well, even repairing a plug lead with a safety pin provided by his passenger. He cornered on two wheels, thinking this was the way to do it. Undoubtedly, he lost a lot of time.

Laird's Red was victorious, soundly whipping Taylor's Norton and going on to set a new 10 lap speed record at 56.05 mph! This effort went a long way in proving the advantage of using a supercharger on Red. Before the next race in a month's time, a three speed gearbox was installed in Red by George Goodall at the Morgan Factory. The new "D" box contained a set of close ratio gears. Three of these special sets were made up for the Morgans and one set was installed in the Rhodes' trike. The third set was obtained by Cyril Hale.

Henry was prepared for action with Red on May 18, 1935 at Donington for the 10 Mile Race. The 1096 cc water cooled JAP was breathing through an Amal TT attached to the Zoller blowing 18 pounds with a 1200 main jet and the clip in the top notch of the needle. Number one cylinder ran a c.r. of 6.1:1, and number two at 5.6:1.

Beginning at the back of the pack for the start, the Lairds advanced to the lead by the end of lap one. They were really ahead by the end of the second lap. Henry and Richard were still leading by a comfortable margin in lap three when a rear main bearing broke. During practice they had run a lap at 62.02 mph, and during the race ran the fastest lap at 60.19 mph in a time of 2 min 33 3/5 seconds. Taylor's Norton sidecar won the race at 56.16 mph, breaking Laird's ten lap record in the process.

Many famous personalities either made a name for themselves at Donington, or at least attempted to do so: Freddie Dixon, the marvelous tuner and driver of a 1935 cc Riley; R.T. Horton and his MG Magnette; and E.V. *Ebby* Ebblewhite, a starter at Donington as well as at the Brooklands course.

An interesting note concerns Richard Laird, Henry's brother and tireless passenger for many of the races with Red. An advertisement for the Brough Superior motorcycle in their catalogue by George Brough in 1935 proudly listed three categories. Fastest Racing Machine – Eric Fernihough – SS 100 Brough Superior. Fastest Touring Machine – Richard Laird on his ridden-on-the-road-every-day 1150 Special. Fastest Sidecar Machine – Eric Fernihough – SS 100. It seems that Richard was a keen motorcyclist in his own right and also a close friend of George Brough.

Several innovations at Donington were presented in 1935 including a lady's race of over 5 laps, but women still were not allowed to ride as passengers in racing machines. The course was widened at Coppice Farm allowing more than enough room for two cars to pass. This set the stage for a 300 mile Grand Prix Event.

Back at Brooklands on May 25, 1935 for the BMCRC "Cup Day" event, Red was now fitted with a special 80 X 107 mm aluminum-bronze crankcase 1084 cc JTOR. According to *Rastas* Lomas, who spent a lot of time working on Red and Yellow, there were three sets of bronze cases made up by E.C.E. *Barry* Baragwanath. One set went to Red. A second set was installed in Noel Pope's Brough for an attempt at world's records. The third set of bronze cases went in the Sumner brothers' car, but was later transferred to John Barton-Hall's Hardy Special.

Several people were involved in the development of Red's bronze engine including Stan Greening who was the Chief Technical Advisor at the J.A. Prestwich firm. K.L. Grieves made the connecting rods. Cast iron barrels were used and a pair of special Baronia bronze heads were later cast by Duncans in Chesterfield. Harry Lomas polished the ports at Melfords. This was sometime after he had concluded employment with McEvoy.

On May 25 at Brooklands, Red used the special bronze JTOR air cooled engine, a TT Amal and 1200 main, but a reduced pressure to 14 pounds from the Zoller. During practice the blower sprocket came off because it was insufficiently tightened. It was welded in place, but after three quarters of a lap refused to stay in place. The press stated, "Laird's Morgan, of course, is colossally fast, but even he cannot conjure mph out if it when the blower stops going 'round."

Tom Rhodes also raced that day with his JTOR engine tuned by Booker and Millington. He finished in third for the 3 lap outer circuit handicap and won the 10 lap outer circuit handicap with a speed of 98.62 mph.

At Donington on June 10, 1935, Laird entered Red in the 25 Mile Passenger Handicap, event number 4. He had reinstalled the water cooled 1096 JAP with the rear main bearing now repaired and was using the Zoller. Laird's supercharged Morgan had to give the other entries 10 seconds a lap. Laird's cornering was magnificent. At the "U" he entered the first part slowly and then brought his Morgan round in a couple of short bursts. The prospects looked good, but no! The clutch oiled up from leakage at the spigot bearing. Henry promised himself not to oil it in the future.

On June 26, 1935, Red was back at Brooklands running with the water cooled 1096 JAP and supercharg-

Brooklands June 26, 1935, Red at speed

er. His passenger was Bill Clarke of HRD Vincent fame on this warm, fine day. They entered the 5 and 10 lap Mountain Races. One lap around was 1.17 miles. Running with gear ratios of 9.1, 6.5:1 and 4.1, they determined that 4:1 was too high for *the Mountain* since they could only manage a 4th place in the 10 lap event.

The Morgan Factory sponsored team returned to Brooklands on July 20, 1935 for the LCC Relay Races, the cars wearing Number 3. For three Morgan trikes, that seemed entirely appropriate.

The LCC this year, for the Fifth Relay Race, made a big effort to encourage the inter-club spirit of friendly competition, especially since there was no inter-club meeting at Brooklands. Club secretaries were invited to submit entries and to form teams which would reflect the name of the club in the program. At the same time, of course, private entries would be welcome.

General regulations remained the same as the previous year, although modified in order to make the race simpler. For example: the driver arriving in the pit would not have to leave his car to hand over the token. He could simply hand the token from his driver's seat to the next driver.

In previous years, the Relay Race had always attracted a magnificent field. In 1932, for instance, there were no less than 87 cars forming 29 teams!

The LCC strived for the lowest possible entry fee. However, the race needed to be an economical proposition, so fees went up in 1935. For club members, the entry fee was 9 pounds, 9 shillings per team; 1 pound 1 shilling was charged for registration, and 2 pounds for insurance (third party risks for up to 10,000 pounds per car). As an offset against this, a more attractive prize list was offered which included a purse to the winning entrant of not less than 50 pounds (instead of the less than 25 pounds offered previously).

The Morgan Team featured Henry in Red as the "A" car running with the 1084 cc bronze crankcase air cooled engine, but without the Zoller. Tom Rhodes was the "B" car in his JAP machine. Clive Lones had the "C" designation with his water cooled 750 JAP engine.

G.R. Hartwell's MG Magnette passing Laird in Red at Brooklands

Laird had installed two track type Amals with a $1\frac{1}{8}$ choke, an 800 jet in No. 1 and 900 in No. 2 using Shell N4 fuel. The compression ratios were 9.8:1 and 10.2:1.

Two other Morgans entered were those of Joe Huxham and Martin Soames. Joe had become good friends with Henry Laird and was persuaded to try a Zoller on his MX2 engine. According to Joe, this was done a month before the race under combined influence from Henry and Flower's Bitter! As

Red at the 1935 JCC Relay Races at Brooklands

Joe told the story, "The performance on the road was terrific. So it was on Brooklands until we came off the banking and on to the railway straight for the second time. Then the front piston burnt a hole in its crown and welded itself to the cylinder bore. I had a standard air cooled Matchless with dry sump lubrications. Henry had a pukka racing JAP wet sump and air cooled unit... Mr. Heather (the head of Matchless) should have had me 'put away.' Tom Bryant (my business partner and good friend) and I worked like 'the devil' stripping and reassembling, fitting extra oil leads, boring out jets, etc. etc. Sammy Lee of Martlets kept turning up with new pistons, each with about $^1/_8$" more clearance than the previous ones, and much help and advice was given by those two grand sports, Minnie and Granville Grenfell, but all to no avail. After two laps the same thing happened again and I had to leave the model by the Hawker sheds and run back to the pits in order to hand the brassard to the next driver in the team. As if to add insult to injury, I was so winded when I got in that I found myself quite incapable of dealing with the personal refueling that my pit attendants had kindly anticipated I should need."

Weybridge near Brooklands, July 1935. Red gets a tow from a Sunbeam returning from the Relay Races

Joe Huxham did eventually resolve the problems when running his Morgan with the Zoller. He had fun competing against sidecars in grass track racing at Ringwood and Shaftesbury. Although he never won a race, he secured several second and third place finishes in those events.

The Morgan of Martin Soames was in another mixed team, running with a JTOR big JAP in a trike which had been exhibited on the show stand at the 1930 Olympia event. The original owner sold Soames the car and he used it for two years on the road before giving it a special treatment for racing. Robin Jackson and Barry Baragwanath worked on the chassis and engine and it was fitted with light weight Dunlop wheels. This racer was lapping over 90 mph with just a single carburetor. The prediction was that it would have done over 100 with dual Amal carburetors.

Laird was the first driver to take the track and was soon lapping at over 93 miles per hour using a rubber band to hold the throttle open. Bumpy Brooklands concrete took a toll and after about 17 laps both of Red's bronze sliding axles broke. He would replace them with a set of steel sliders made by Brasser Smith's in Derby before any more track work.

Rhodes was next out and completed 43 laps, managing laps in the 90s. Lones' engine broke its timing gear, thus ending the Morgan team's efforts.

The winners of the Relay Race were the Singers driven by Barnes, Langley and Bicknell with 85.13 mph after a 40 min start. Second place was awarded to a mixed team of cars; Watson's Frazer Nash, Barker's Lagonda and Powell's MG with an average speed of 77.69 mph after a 51 min start. Eleven other teams finished. The Aston Martin team had the highest average at 89.86 mph. Bringing up the rear were Hartwell's MG, Huxham's Morgan, and Hendy's Singer team with 77.13 mph.

This event closed an important chapter in Morgan racing history. It marked the last time a factory sponsored team would race under the Morgan banner in a Relay Race at Brooklands.

Returning to Donington Park on August 5, 1935 for Monday Bank Holiday, Henry and Richard fitted Red with the air cooled 1084 cc bronze engine and the Zoller. They struggled to get the engine to run without missing by installing Lodge BR19 plugs in the number one cylinder and BR29 in the second, setting the Bosch magneto to fire the first cylinder at $^5/_8$" before top dead center. An Amal with a 109 needle and 1100 main jet regulated 50/50 fuel. Compression ratios were set to 6.2:1 on number one and 5.65:1 on the number two cylinder on this very hot day.

Yellow at a check point during the 1935 ISDT in Bavaria

Starting with a 100 second handicap in the unlimited passenger event, Red really flew for the first two laps. One of the laps was timed at 2 min 40 seconds. Then the Pilgrim oil pump failed and oil wasn't delivered to vital parts. Piston clearances were 12 thousands on the skirt, 16 below the bottom ring, and 24 thousands on the top, and the number two cylinder still seized. Disappointed but undaunted, the Lairds would spend many hours adjusting the carburetor and trying various engine compression ratios to find a racing optimum.

The International Six Days' Trial took place on September 9, 1935 at Oberstdorf, Germany. It was the longest Six Days held to date, covering a distance of 1,650 miles with a dozen or more time checks a day – one about every 20 or 25 miles. The official schedule recommended that participants keep speeds between 20 and 34 miles per hour depending on their type of machine. As competitors are prone to doing, as soon as they cleared one check, they drove as fast as they could in case a puncture or other problem developed, figuring they could make repairs and still reach the next check on time. Driven by this fear, most competitors habitually averaged around 40 mph over roads which were unsuitable for such speeds. Very few entrants finished with undamaged vehicles.

Prior to the trial, the Morgan factory made some modifications to the body on Yellow. The battered beetle back body was removed and thrown on the scrap heap but later claimed by Derek Evans who took it home to Worcester to be preserved as a priceless relic. Derek was a lifelong Morgan enthusiast and a Morgan employee. He was a next door neighbor to Bob Currie, the novice motorcyclist who would explore an interest in Red at a later date.

A much more practical boat shaped tail was fitted to Yellow with a flat slab top which gave room to carry two spare tires. It is suspected the body came from George Goodall's old trials car. The raised body sides gave easier access to the rear wheel. At the same time, the rear suspension was improved with the friction damper and two speeder fork suspension recycled from Red when it was converted to a gearbox model. Yellow was repainted in the customary primrose color and looked very smart. This, no doubt, appeased the Morgan family who seemed a bit embarrassed by Yellow's tatty and run down condition despite being earned through trials.

An official ISDT Nazi entry, Bergmuller, on a 596 cc Victoria sidecar outfit made an outstanding climb up one of the hills. The Lairds then followed even faster with a scary ride for Barbara. She was leaning out of the trike in both directions facing road side drop offs of 1,000 feet on nearly every hairpin turn. The Lairds had to average over 32 mph on this hill which rarely had any straights over 50 yards in length.

Yellow was fitted with Red's frequently used water cooled engine and Zoller. They ran smoothly until Thursday when the front of the Morgan dropped into two enormous ruts, hanging up the chassis. The front suspension and sliding axle were damaged. The front brakes were out of service. It took Henry and Barbara 59 minutes, working like Titans, to drag the car out, prop the front end up on a petrol can, and replace the broken slider. One more minute lost and they would have been disqualified with no chance of earning any award. As it turned out, they were the only British passenger machine to finish.

The German teams emerged with flying colors. The

Czechoslovakian team was leading by 3 marks over the German team at Fussen, site of the final speed test, but one of their team members pulled out. This let the German team win the event and secure the International Silver Vase.

One editorial opinion in the press stated that, "Once again it has to be admitted that British riders were unprepared for their task. Germany has now won the Trophy for three years in succession. If Britain is to win it back, she must take a leaf out of the German book. The machines must be produced for the purpose in hand – each designed and made with all the thoroughness of a TT winner. The riders, too, must be prepared; they must know their machines, be able to overcome any trouble in the minimum time and know the course."

An extract from the issue of *Das Motorrad* of September 9, 1935 perhaps says it best, "There were a number of unique machines in the 'Six Days'. By far the strangest was the Morgan – this time there was only one of them. At the start of any special test the driver leapt out with an enormous handle, stuck it into the side of the body and wound his gramophone up. It looked funny, but go, the Morgan went like hell (Donnerwetter), always kept up to time and 'sat down' astonishingly well on the loose stuff. He only lost marks owing to the front brake anchorage shearing, which took some time to repair. He did not even get a 'bronze', but was nevertheless able to show in the speed test at the end that the machine was still in good order and his speed was higher than that of many of the solos."

zine of August 8, 1935, "I would be glad of a small space in your correspondence columns to place on record my ideas on the possibilities of supercharged V-twins. There was a paragraph in 'Sports Jottings' recently which implied that it was useless to supercharge a big twin unless the engine was specially built and designed for the job. I myself have been running a supercharged Morgan with a JAP engine of 1927 vintage for some eight months. Apart from a pair of low compression pistons, the engine is absolutely standard in every respect. During the winter months the machine ran through practically all the big open trials, and in between times was used for traveling to and from work and for holiday transport. The same engine, in identical trim, was transferred into the machine I use for racing (Red) and has succeeded in lapping Donington at over 62 mph on petrol-benzole. Further, it was run in a Mountain race at Brooklands and several laps were covered at a speed in excess of 67 mph. If anyone doubts the truth of these remarks I am prepared to match my supercharged trials Morgan, running on petrol-benzole, against any un-supercharged three-wheeler or Shelsley Special running on the same fuel."

Two months later on October 22, 1935 Henry and Barbara, with encouragement and accompaniment from Joe Huxham and Tom Bryant, took Red to Brooklands. They were out to break records! The Morgan had the bronze crankcase JTOR with the Zoller and Martlett pistons as set up for the August meeting at Donington. The trike was tuned with Lodge BR 29 plugs fired by a Lucas B magneto. An Amal with a 109 needle jet and 1400 main metered

During the ISDT, Yellow competed well over the many mountain passes. Michael McEvoy remarked, "Laird had never realized the full beauties of a supercharger until he reached an altitude of 8,000 feet or so at which height air shows a marked reluctance to being sucked in through one's carburetor intake."

Henry Laird wrote a treatise in the press about supercharging a standard big twin in *Light Car* maga-

Yellow in rally guise. Note the knobby tires for trials work

Henry and Barbara Laird with Red at Brooklands, October 22, 1935. A happy moment during the record breaking attempts

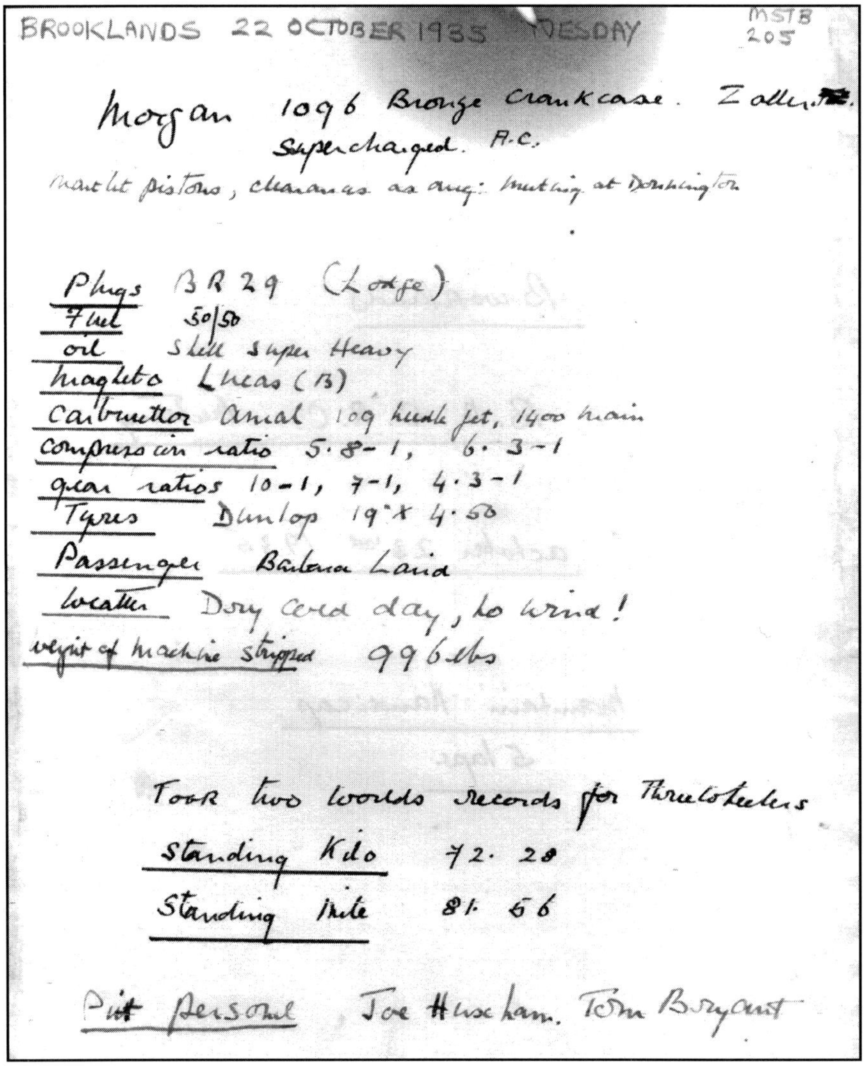

BROOKLANDS 22 OCTOBER 1935 TUESDAY MSTB 205

Morgan 1096 Bronze Crankcase. Zoller. Supercharged. A.C.
Martlet pistons, clearances as aug: meeting at Donington

Plugs BR 29 (Lodge)
Fuel 50/50
oil Shell super Heavy
Magneto Lucas (B)
Carburettor Amal 109 needle jet, 1400 main
Compression ratio 5·8-1, 6·3-1
gear ratios 10-1, 7-1, 4·3-1
Tyres Dunlop 19" x 4·50
Passenger Barbara Laird
Weather Dry cold day, no wind!
weight of machine stripped 996 lbs

Took two worlds records for Threewheelers
Standing Kilo 72·28
Standing Mile 81·56

Pit personnel Joe Huscham. Tom Bryant

The October 22, 1935 page from Barbara Laird's track notebook

the 50/50 fuel blend of petrol-benzole. Running Dunlop 19 x 450 tires, the machine's weight was 996 pounds with the front mudguards removed.

Barbara passengered for an attempt at the standing start mile and kilometer world's records for piston driven three wheelers. The weather was dry and cold with no wind and Red seemed eager to prove itself. According to Barbara, an electrical tape timing was conducted in both directions before a record could be sanctioned. Red was up to the challenge and continued to run spectacularly well. The Standing Start Kilometer World's Records were taken at 72.288 mph, beating H. Moritz' (DKW-Moritz) previous record by 1 1/2 mph. Henry and Barbara went on to take the Standing Start Mile Record at 81.568 mph, beating Gwenda Stewart's previous record by 1 mph. The Association Internationale des Automobile Clubs Reconnus (AIACR), which, in 1947, became the Federation Internationale de l'Automobile (FIA) recognized class figures internationally – therefore the Laird's accomplishments were World Records for piston-driven three wheelers. It was a glorious day indeed and much celebrating followed!

The Lairds didn't rest for long. They were back at Brooklands the following day on October 23 for the BMCRC Meet of the Year. This time Red was set up as the previous day with compression ratios of 5.8:1 and 6.3:1 and gear ratios of 10:1, 7:1 and 4.3:1. The weather was fine and dry. Tom Bryant passengered. Laird's handicap was 47 seconds. They won the Five Lap Mountain Race (about 5.75 miles) and set a new cycle-car record of 5 min 31.8 seconds with a speed of 63.44 mph, demolishing the previous three wheeler record by 18.4 seconds. More celebrating followed this second consecutive day of achieving new records!

Before the year was out Henry went to print again, this time in the *Light Car* of December 13, 1935 with "A Racing Driver's Opinions" in the Readers' Opinions column of the magazine. The content will be obvious without stating the comments of Mr. Esmond in an earlier issue. Henry had this to say, "Evidently Mr. W.J. Esmond cannot appreciate the fact that, for performance, the three-wheeler is the cheapest and safest passenger vehicle on the road.

Red after setting the World's Records for the SS Mile and Kilometer for piston driven three wheelers

Any vehicle will skid if driven too fast in the wrong place; Mr. Esmond may have got into difficulties on corners because he does not properly appreciate that the good road holding of a three-wheeler tends to make him corner faster than when driving an 8 hp 'glass house on wheels'. In connection with fuel consumption, surely the cc of an engine must be taken into consideration. It is true, as Mr. Esmond says, that the 8 hp three-wheelers do not average 42-45 mpg – they do better than that! An ordinary 1,100 cc three-wheeler covers 35-40 mpg. How many four-wheelers of this cc can equal that figure? They are the exception rather than the rule, and a 1,100 cc four-wheeler of equivalent performance usually does only 25 mpg. If Mr. Esmond can find a suitable 8 hp four-wheeler the sooner he gets it the better, or he may prejudice prospective 'tricyclists' and rob them of a pleasure they should not miss." Henry Laird, Derby.

The Morgan 4/4 with Coventry Climax 1090 cc engine received Morgan factory support in 1936

On Boxing Day, the 21st running of the London-Exeter Trial took place. H.F.S. Morgan was an entrant in the veteran class. Perhaps in celebration of his 1910 participation, he drove the first 4/4 (four wheels, four cylinders) production model and won a Premier Award with it! Earlier this Coventry Climax engined car made an appearance in July at Brooklands. The front body work on the 4/4 more closely resembled that of an F-model than a four wheeler Morgan. It carried registration WP 7490, the same as on the earlier F-model in which Peter Morgan learned to drive on the grounds of his father's home.

The three wheelers for the London-Exeter were those of Henry Laird, Jim Goodall and Joe Huxham. Jim won a silver medal. Joe also won a silver and the Simms Hill Trophy. Henry retired with no award.

As history recorded, 1936 marked a new beginning for Morgan racing. The Morgan four wheeler gained factory support for events. Tom Rhodes ended his racing career and purchased a public house in Wales. Clive Lones joined the four wheeler contingent by modifying his three wheeler. He kept the body in its normal shape but modified the drive train with a solid GN chain driven rear axle, quarter-elliptic rear springs and radius arms to the bevel box. The two rear wheels now ran outside the three wheeler tail. He named this new creation *Tiger Cat* and entered several popular sprint and hill climbs with success, running with both the 731 and 996 cc air cooled engines. With only front brakes, he must have been somewhat hindered at events.

Wintry weather prevailed in February 1936 for the Colmore Trophy Car Trial held in the Cotswolds by the Sutton Coldfield and North Birmingham Automobile Club (Sunbac). There were 125 drivers from promoting clubs which included the MG Car Club, the Singer Motor Car Club, the Scottish Sporting Car Club, the Light Car Club and the N.W. London Motor Club. Out of the list of entries, 10 didn't start and only 82 qualified as finishers. Just 27 recorded no penalties. Laird drove the 1092 cc McEvoy Special for the 10 AM start at the Fish Inn near Broadway. The drivers set out in pairs at three minute intervals. The day began with only a biting wind, but the weather soon turned to snow, covering the higher ground. The route ran from Broadway, through Stanton Hill, and on to Stanway. At Stanway Hill, where a restart test was held, a dozen drivers lost marks. Fifteen took more than the allotted 7 seconds. One of the Singers broke an axle shaft. Above the test, five others failed in an easy observed section. Laird raced on in the McEvoy Special, having one of the best times. It was onto Kineton, a difficult obstacle, where there were failures even among the more experienced drivers.

A driving test near Guiting, despite rain and sleet, saw many fine performances. Henry Laird and A.H. Langley had the best of these. The drivers then went on to West Down, Mill Lane and another driving test of a steep hill near Syde. An easy climb up Greenway Lane near Birdlip indicated the final control.

H. Symons in a Frazer Nash BMW was the chief competition for Laird who seemed to be in top form. On Stancomb, Laird went one up by climbing in 18.3 sec against Symons' 21.3 sec time. Both climbed Nailsworth Ladder, but when they got to Ham Mill, Symons found a rut, stopped and went two down. When they reached Jupiter, neither could climb it, although Symons reached a higher point. If only Symons could score on Cold Slad, he could half the match, but it didn't happen. Laird made a good climb and Symons stopped cold. The Colmore Trophy for the best performance was awarded to Henry Laird.

Despite the victory in the McEvoy Special, the Lairds remained faithful to three wheelers and continued using both Yellow and Red. They entered Yellow with the Zoller in the Bemrose Trial in early March, 1936. This annual trial was sponsored by the Derby and Donington Motor Cycle Club.

The weather was excellent for this 90 mile course which started from Craner's Garage on the London road at Derby and ended a few miles from Buxton in the Peak District. The course contained nearly every type of surface which any trials' organization could hope to include in a challenging trials event. Several machines got stuck in thick mud and no one completed the course without losing marks.

On one particular hill, the prospect was simply impossible that Yellow would get up and the officials allowed the Lairds to roll back and tackle the hill again. They made a clean climb on the second attempt, but it must be noted that as a spectacle likely to produce heart failure due to over excitement, it took the cake! On another hill they had to use plenty of throttle to get up. Their spinning rear wheel carved a deep and wide lane in the muck as they ploughed through without stopping. A 348 BSA, ridden by L. Eyre, used this to advantage and followed in their track, making the only clean climb up to that point. The Lairds turned in a magnificent performance, losing only 10 marks, and were awarded the Syston Cup. They also took home the Derby Club Cup in the closed club awards division.

The Wye Valley Trial took place on March 28, 1936 and Yellow wasonce again entered. Reporters stated that the Lairds provided the biggest thrill of the afternoon on Pumpkins Hill. They came up fairly fast, leaped from step to step, and hardly seemed to touch all three wheels at any one time. Barbara performed her usual weight shifting, hung out over the rear wheel as required and gave the spectators a thrill. To the crowd, Yellow appeared to be close to going out of control, but with Henry at the wheel, that possibility was extremely remote. Two other Morgans driven by W.A. Jim Goodall and F. Williams, were not as lucky. Mr. Williams was quite spectacular, but not the equal of the Lairds. Mr. Goodall hit a particular deep ledge with the left front wheel, bent it under the chassis and had to retire on the spot! Henry and Barbara only lost 6 marks and received a First Class award.

For the March 18, 1936 issue of *Motor Cycling* magazine, A. Mentice (Mark III), was invited by Henry Laird to spend a weekend in the Derby area and give Red a road test. On Saturday they drove over to the McEvoy works where the racer was kept and prepared it for the test the following day. Sunday morning arrived and after Mentice was given some instructions by Henry, Barbara Laird went along as his passenger.

His comments were typical of those expressed by fans of the record breaking machine and he was also a little nervous during his first attempt at driving a supercharged Morgan racer, especially in the company of Barbara who was used to being expertly driven by Henry. Mentice observed the spartan dash panel which had a pressure gauge for the supercharger and the bare minimum of instruments, even less than the standard Morgan. At that time Red was fitted with a foot accelerator. The blower was mounted by aluminum plates on the lower front chassis tubes near the left front wheel. The side cranking hole in the body could no longer be used for starting since a gearbox had been installed. Henry had to push start the trike. The engine fired after about three yards. The lusty JAP gave a hearty crackle despite the restrictions of the two Brooklands silencers.

Mentice was surprised at the engine's smoothness and how the Morgan would run along smoothly at low speeds in top gear and accelerate without hesitation. On the open road, he pressed the foot accelerator hard and shot down the road "like an arrow from a bow" – a "white-knuckle" experience. He got the speed up to that of a standard Morgan and still hadn't shifted into third! When the change was made into top gear, and more pressure applied on the throttle, Mentice found the acceleration was almost as good as when in second.

Mentice and Barbara headed across the Derbyshire hills toward Winster near Matlock, where the roads had little traffic. Closely following behind them was Henry Laird in the supercharged McEvoy Special. Mentice

Barbara, Henry and A. Mentice road testing Red, January 1936. Note the dealer's plate

Red's dashboard showing the drip oil feed, ignition off switch and rubber band holding the choke lever open

Red at speed during road testing with Henry and Barbara Laird, January 1936

took Red on a nice down hill stretch with a left turn at the bottom, and as he down shifted the throttle froze open. He quickly reached for the kill button on the dash and shut off the engine. With a bit of a tail wag on the snow, Red had come around the corner as if on rails. From then on, proceeding to where they could get the carburetor unfrozen, he drove with the kill switch, causing black smoke to blow out the exhausts. Henry, who was following, knew what was happening and commended Mentice on his good driving. We're not sure what Barbara's comments were.

The test article noted that during the racing season, no icing problems were experienced since the weather was warmer. This exhilarating Sunday morning test drive proved to *Mark III* that Red was challenging and fun. But his fun was just beginning, as Henry took the wheel in the afternoon to demonstrate what Red could do. Mark crouched down in the passenger's side as the trike whipped around tight corners with the tires squealing and the engine screaming with high acceleration. It was a ride which made him appreciate to the fullest those driving skills possessed by Henry in his handling of the Red Morgan racer.

Henry Laird with Michael Faraday, Barbara's brother, Donington Park, Easter 1936

While trial work continued with Yellow, Red received some modifications. The position of the Zoller was always a problem. The mounting low down on the chassis near the left front wheel was not a warm location and the carburetor often ingested loose road material. Since Red was fitted with the air cooled bronze cased JTOR engine, the radiator was no longer needed and was removed.

Henry had Red delivered to the Star Hotel in Worcester, not far from the Morgan Factory. It was collected by Derek Evans who drove it to the factory where the cowl was modified and shaped into a slope and the fuel tank reshaped to fit under it. The oil tank access hole on the left side remained in the original position. Two pieces of heavy 2" angle iron, measuring 15.75" and 13.5" long with a .25" thickness were welded across the top chassis tubes just behind the engine. This became the platform for the supercharger and carburetor. In this new position, no icing could possibly occur and the chances of sucking track debris through the carburetor intake became slim.

Donington Park, April 13, 1936. The first race following the cowl modification. Note the JAP engine with chain drive on the Zoller supercharger

In addition to the canvas covered hump over the rear wheel, installed earlier, slots were cut through the floor boards allowing the beetle back to be dropped 2 inches over the chassis, lowering the center of gravity. Two grab handles were mounted on the body. One just behind the passenger's wind scallop and the other beyond the passenger seat. The racing passenger grasped one or both handles while leaning out of the trike to transfer weight to the left front wheel when cornering, forcing that wheel back onto the road surface. These acrobatics were common for *the monkey*, or the racing motorcycle sidecar passenger.

The chassis was also tuned. Double *flying wires* or chassis supports were fitted into special lugs located near the ends of the top cross tubes. The width between center pins became 46.50" at the bottom and 46.25" at the top. The top cross tubes were bent back one inch to improve the steering geometry, or handling. The distance between the front tire centers now measured 55 inches, an increase of five inches.

April 13, 1936, Easter Monday meet at Donington Park

A metal box measuring 9 by 5.25 by 6.5 inches was mounted behind the driver's seat cushion on the bulkhead and became an oil reservoir. It had a filler cap on top and two drain taps on the side and bottom with copper tubes. One ran into the gearbox which allowed it to be replenished quickly. The other was directed over the drive chain to keep it lubed.

The braking system had been modified earlier using rear drums on the front hubs which were stronger than the factory front drums. The front backing plates were opened up and a wire screen brazed over the front opening. With holes drilled into the rear of the plates to allow for air flow, cooling was greatly assisted. Newton shocks remained in place on the front while two Hartford friction dampers were installed on the rear, one either side of the wheel. The ends of the rear forks had been slotted to facilitate speedy wheel removal. The rear axle could be slipped straight back and off the trike in a hurry after the chain and brake cable were disconnected.

Henry's ingenuity created other modifications on the front braking controls. A dual pulley system was incorporated with two 2.37 by .31 inch wheels, measuring 2.87 inches between centers clamped onto a sliding metal lever on the front end of the torque tube. The front brake cable, in one continuous strand, wound through the pulleys. A threaded rod of 11.34 inches ran from the front pulley lever to a yoke and clamp in front of the gearshift lever. This yoke had a handle attached for the front braking system. This cable and pulley modification resulted in a positive, smooth action. The rear brake cable was operated by the foot pedal.

The front wheel hubs were machined to accommodate Timkin tapered roller bearings, replacing the .25 inch loose ball bearings and cup and cone arrangement that was the factory standard on all Morgan two speeder front hubs.

When the modifications were completed, Henry and Barbara traveled to Malvern Link to collect Red from the Morgan Factory. Henry was very pleased with the results. However, when Barbara saw the sloping front cowl her comment was not printable. Today, the sloping cowl looks quite streamlined and modern – perhaps even art-deco. In the 1930s, things were looked at differently, especially from Barbara's viewpoint.

Now that Red sported a new cowl and the radiator had been discarded, it could only run with the 1084 cc JTOR air cooled engine or one of some other manufacture.

Red's race debut with its new sleek sloping cowl was on April 13, 1936 at Donington for the 10 Lap Sidecar Handicap Event. The 1084 bronze crankcase JAP was running with Lodge BR 29 plugs, a 50/50 fuel mixture and Amal carburetor. The pit personal were Barbara Laird, Mona Swank, Kim Collett, S. Clowes, Albert Kheene and M.A. McEvoy. The sun barely

Edwin Charles Ellis Baragwanath, the JAP tuning expert, chatting with Henry at Brooklands, May 1936

made an appearance as Henry rolled to the starting grid with Richard as passenger, but Red basked in the attention of spectators and competitors alike.

Henry had to give 60 seconds to the 500 cc sidecar outfits, but Red ran well five laps into the race with times averaging around 2 min 42 seconds. He looked like the probable race winner until the oil pump failed, forcing withdrawal.

The Easter Donington Meet had 10 entries for the sidecar class but only seven actually started. Ever since sidecar racing was introduced at Donington, Kim Collett of Oxford had held the undisputed edge. But this day he lost to not only one individual, but to two entries in races for three wheelers and sidecars. In the class for 500 cc machines, H. Tozer beat him by 50 yards. In the unlimited class, he was beaten by Laird's Morgan. Red had a bad start but forged ahead on the third lap with such effort that he won the event at 55 mph in 27 min 59.8 seconds. Kim Collett's Norton sidecar placed second and the sidecar of W.H. Rose took third. The fastest time of the day was posted by H.L. Daniell on a Norton at 65 mph.

Henry was again a great crowd pleaser, driving Red in a very polished manner, remaining calm and refusing to become flustered in the congested traffic. The changes made to Red seemed to work out well, and the press commented favorably on the new sloping cowl which became Laird's trademark.

The Travers Trophy Trial was held in late April and was just over 100 miles running from Newcastle to Alston in Cumberland and involved some precipitous hills in the highest part of England. The event was an open motorcycle trial, but since car entries were allowed by members of the Newcastle and the DMC, Henry Laird entered the 1086 cc McEvoy Special which had a locked differential. This was his entry since the supercharger had been moved from Yellow to Red for the Easter meet at Donington. The event received the official support of motorcycle manufacturers. There was some controversy since no restrictions barred cars from having a locked differential, although sidecar wheel drive was not allowed.

Several people were chagrined when Henry ran the course without losing a mark on observation. There were a total of eight clean sheets and a run-off was decided by a braking test which Henry posted at 71.38. The results were that Henry won the 200 guinea Travers Trophy. D.K. Mansell was the only sidecar to finish without losing any marks and received the White Eagle Trophy. The event concluded with suggestions that the Centre should make drastic alterations to the rules if they hoped to get the continued support from motorcycle manufacturers at future trials.

Henry and Barbara Laird aired their views in the press stating that they thought it quite wrong that a four wheeler should compete against solo motorcycles and sidecars for the same trophy. "Also, it is agreed that if a sidecar wheel drive is barred on sidecar outfits, it is quite unfair that a four wheeler should be allowed a solid axle. Our Morgan being out of action and having studied the regulations as they were laid down, we should have been foolish to fit a differential to our four wheeler when there was a good chance of retaining a clean sheet without one. The regulations should certainly be modified, but the fact remains they were there for everyone to read and, presumably, it was thought impossible for a four wheeler to win against all comers. We have always contended that a suitable four wheeler can go anywhere a motorcycle can, provided there is sufficient room. We proved this to our own satisfaction some time ago by climbing the Coniston side of Walna Scar unassisted. Anybody who has ridden a motorcycle will endorse our opinion that a four wheeler is 'easy money' compared with a solo, sidecar, or three wheeler."

Red was back on the track in May for the Brooklands Meeting and the 1084 cc engine now had Baronia bronze cylinder heads. These heads were manufactured to improve cooling in the valve seat areas. Red was running an Amal with a 113 needle jet and 1300 main regulating 50/50 Shell fuel. Richard was passengering and Barry Baragwanath was present to offer help and advice. Bad vibrations were in the air that day and a broken piston occurred in the number one cylinder after only 1 $^{1}/_{2}$ laps.

On June 1, 1936, Henry and Richard went back to Donington for the Whit Monday Meeting, entering Red in the 25 Mile Passenger Handicap Event. One of eight starters, they were in the company of Cyril Hale in his MX4 racer and Kim Collett with his Brough Superior JTOR sidecar outfit.

The Lairds started well, but had to retire after one lap when the spring link came out of the supercharger drive chain, disengaging the unit. The Brough side car turned over. Cyril Hale went on to take second place.

The organizers of Donington Park at the August Bank Holiday meet on August 3, 1936 made a special ruling limiting the engine capacity to 750 cc for the passenger event. They believed this evened the competition between motorcycles and Morgans. Henry Laird was rather peeved at this and decided that his Morgan should not back down. He borrowed a 500 cc 60-degree Blackburne engine and put it on Red. He bolted on two 1936 TT Amals, ran a 240 jet in cylinder one and a 310 in number two, and fitted a 16 tooth gearbox sprocket. Richard climbed aboard as his passenger and they went for blood on this fine cold day. His support crew consisted of Barbara, M. Swank, P. Swank and J. Clowes.

Things went well for the first seven laps, but on the eighth, he missed a gear change and the Blackburne's main shaft broke. It was later discovered that the shaft was faulty and not Henry's driving. No matter, he was deprived of fully proving his point regarding Morgans being competitive under the new rules.

On August 4, 1936, Henry and Richard took Red back to Donington, again with the 1084 bronze crankcase JAP, Baronia heads, the Zoller and new RR 59 machine forged pistons installed. He set the engine up with Lodge BR 52 plugs and the 1 $^{1}/_{4}$" Amal with a 113 needle and 1400 main jet. This time he ran a 20 tooth gearbox sprocket driving a 4.50 x 19 rear tire. Barbara Laird, in the company of M. Swank, P. Swank and J. Clowes, provided his crew support.

For this 25 Mile Passenger Handicap Race, Taylor's 600 cc Norton sidecar had a 40 second start and came in first. Douglas' 750 cc sidecar had a 35 second start and only beat the Lairds by 10 yards. Henry and

Brooklands, May 1936. Zoller mounted with Amal TT carburetor

August 3, 1936 Donington Park. Richard Laird *hanging out* at Red Gate Corner

August 4, 1936 at Donington for the start of the 25 mile race

Richard took third at 58.43 mph running off scratch. During the race Red's brakes begin fading after two laps but Henry still drove well, gaining 5 seconds on the leader during the last lap by using full throttle down the straight for the first time. Henry stripped down the engine two days later and found it to be in excellent condition. Perhaps all the elements were finally coming together.

The International Six Days' Trial began on September 17, 1936 in Bavaria. Henry and Barbara took Yellow for the event fitted with the Zoller. Unfortunately, Yellow suffered a broken oil pipe and the big end of the JAP began to tighten. Rather than chance blowing the engine, they decided to retire. That afternoon they took the damaged parts into Stuttgart and made the necessary repairs.

Brooklands was the setting on October 10, 1936 for the BMCRC Hutchinson 100, 37 laps of the outer circuit. Henry and Richard Laird took Red out on this cold, dry day. Barbara Laird and Jack Scott were the pit crew.

Red used the 1084 cc bronze crankcase engine and the Baronia bronze heads running dirt track pistons with a clearance of 10 thousand on the skirt. Two track type Amals with 840 and 900 jets regulated 811 Shell fuel. This was a mixture of 80% alcohol and 20% benzole. The compression was raised to 11:1 with the Bosch magneto set to fire number one cylinder at 45-degrees before top dead center. To provide enough fuel for the length of this event, an auxiliary fuel tank was fitted on the floor beneath the passenger's legs. A hand pump was provided to top off the main tank and the overflow tube ran back inside the cockpit. The passenger now had more than balance to occupy his attention.

Richard Laird, in a moment of excitement, pumped too much fuel into the main tank and the overflow went straight into his lap. Finishing the race in a most uncomfortable state, he had to use a silk handkerchief around sensitive parts of his anatomy for several days.

Red ran well for the first 30 laps averaging around 99 mph before the carburetor on the number 2 cylinder came loose and caused the piston to melt. He then had to limp around the circuit on one cylinder but still managed to average 87.99 mph to finish all 37 laps. Out of 36 starters, Henry became one of only 10 riders to finish the event as the last riders were flagged off near dusk.

The event was won by S.H. Goddard on a 246 OK Supreme-JAP in 1 hour, 15 min 51 sec at a speed of 85.87 mph average. Second place went to a Norton rider. Third to a Rudge rider. Fourth through seventh places to other Norton riders. C.K. Mortimer on his 348 Norton was the sixth place winner at 1 hour, 17 min 20 sec averaging 94.50 mph. Henry and Richard Laird secured eighth place with a time of 1 hour 22 min 47 seconds. More importantly, they secured a place in the history books by lapping at 100.61 mph on laps 11, 13, and 16. This effort was enough for

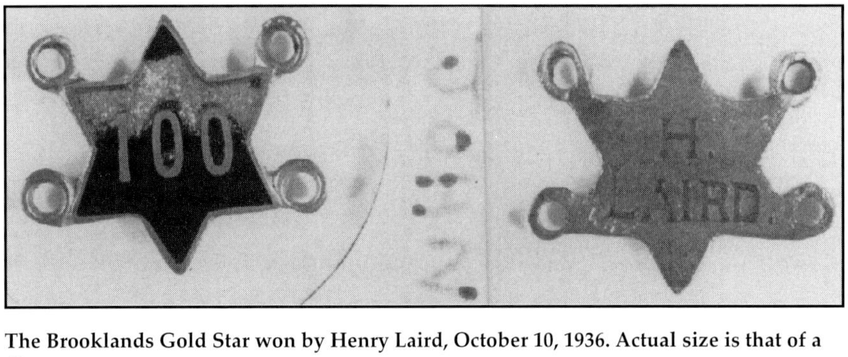

The Brooklands Gold Star won by Henry Laird, October 10, 1936. Actual size is that of a dime

them to be awarded the coveted Brooklands Gold Star. The official timing sheet for Laird which documented the times and speed was signed by A.V. Ebblewhite, clerk of the course.

An historical note is that only three other Morgan drivers were awarded the 100 Mile Brooklands Gold Stars. In 1930, H.C. Lones and R.R. Jackson secured theirs. T.A. Rhodes won his in 1934. The Lairds were in good company.

Richard Laird's last race with Henry and Red was in the 1936 "Hutchinson 100" because he was transferred by his company in March of 1937 to their branch in Shanghai. Between that time and the end of World War II, Richard spent three and a half years in a Japanese POW camp. During one of his bouts of illness, he was able to cheer up his compatriots a little by relating his experience during the "100" when he managed to spill fuel in his lap. Richard did survive as a prisoner and returned to the U.K. during November 1945. Of course, racing in England was totally different by then, and he wouldn't ride in Red again. However, he did ride in Yellow again many years later when Titch Allen took him on a demonstration run at one of the MTWC meets. It's interesting to note that Richard never drove Red and only drove Yellow on one occasion with unpleasant results. He ran into a stone wall and damaged the chassis, but says that Henry didn't get mad.

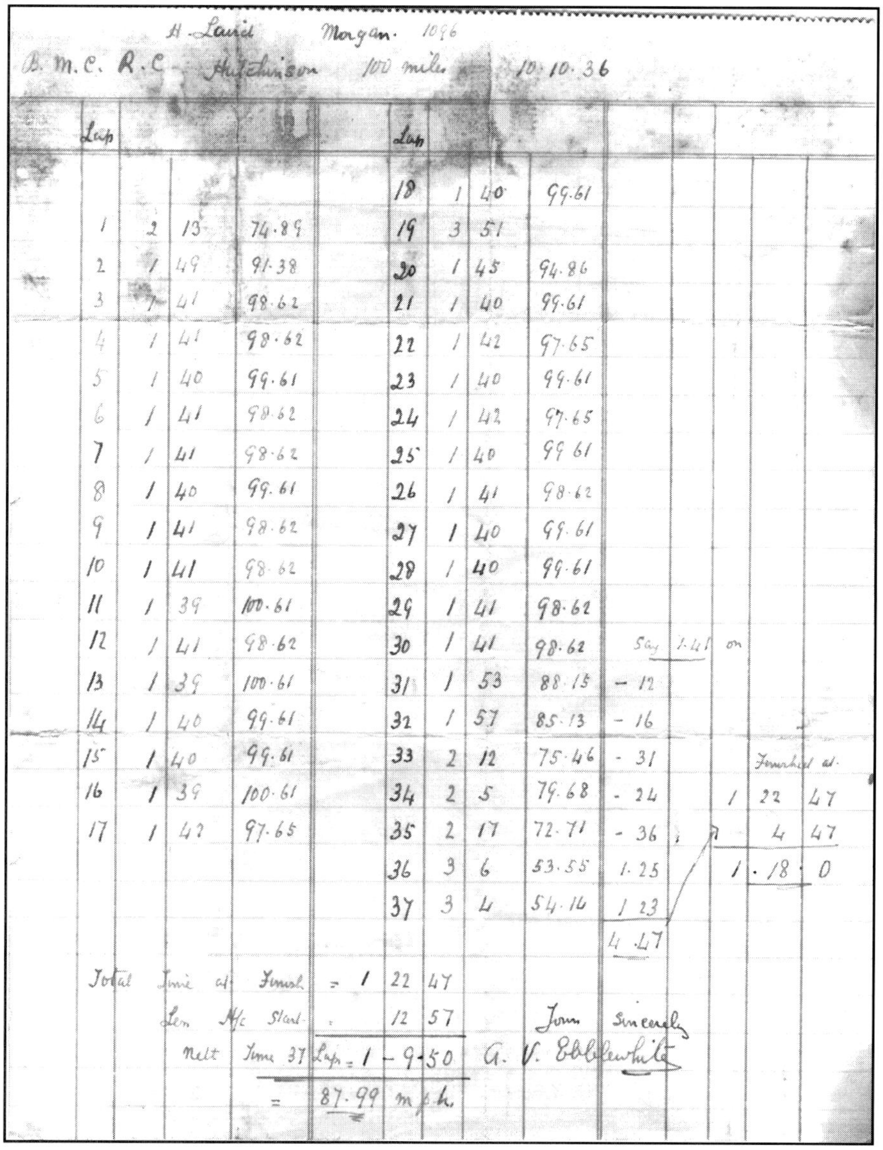
H. Laird Morgan. 1096
B.M.C.R.C. Hutchinson 100 miles 10.10.36

Lap				Lap							
				18	1	40	99.61				
1	2	13	74.89	19	3	51					
2	1	49	91.38	20	1	45	94.86				
3	1	41	98.62	21	1	40	99.61				
4	1	41	98.62	22	1	42	97.65				
5	1	40	99.61	23	1	40	99.61				
6	1	41	98.62	24	1	42	97.65				
7	1	41	98.62	25	1	40	99.61				
8	1	40	99.61	26	1	41	98.62				
9	1	41	98.62	27	1	40	99.61				
10	1	41	98.62	28	1	40	99.61				
11	1	39	100.61	29	1	41	98.62				
12	1	41	98.62	30	1	41	98.62	Say 1.41 on			
13	1	39	100.61	31	1	53	88.15	- 12			
14	1	40	99.61	32	1	57	85.13	- 16			
15	1	40	99.61	33	2	12	75.46	- 31	Finished at.		
16	1	39	100.61	34	2	5	79.68	- 24	1	22	47
17	1	42	97.65	35	2	17	72.71	- 36		4	47
				36	3	6	53.55	1.25	1	.18	0
				37	3	4	54.16	1 23			
								4 47			

Total time at finish = 1 22 47
Less A/c start = 12 57
Nett time 37 laps = 1 - 9 50
= 87.99 m.p.h.
Yours sincerely
A. V. Ebblewhite

The Brooklands lap chart signed by A.V. Ebblewhite, October 10, 1936. Note the speed on laps 11, 13 and 16

Shortly after the Hutchinson 100, Henry took Red back to Brooklands in an attempt to break the outer lap record held by Tommy Rhodes at 103.76 mph. Red was set up basically as it had been for the previous event, but with certain important modifications. The compression was raised to 12.9:1 on the number one cylinder and from 11:1 to 12.4 on number two. The fuel was changed to Racing Shell Ethel and jet sizes in the track type Amals changed from the 840 and 900 to 1500 on both sides. Testing showed this was all right for the number 2 cylinder, but number 1 ran a little too weak so twin float chambers were used. The Bosch magneto timing was changed from 45 to 42 degrees BTDC to better fire the number one piston.

The gear ratio of 3.7:1 proved to be too high for the existing weather conditions which allowed for a strong head wind along the Railway Straight. This ratio was calculated to deliver a top speed of 106 mph at 5400 rpm. The correct gear ratio for the 1 lap record should really guarantee at least 110 mph at 5500 rpm.

After a push start, timing was begun after two laps and continued for an additional two laps. A lap speed of 103 mph was reached but couldn't be improved. The outer lap record was still secure with Tommy Rhodes!

In 1936 Henry and Barbara moved into a new home. Henry transferred Red on the Log Book to 15 Station Rd, Kenilworth, Warwickshire. They celebrated the 1936 holiday season by sending out another of their

Barbara and Henry Laird's 1936 Christmas card

humorous greeting cards which portrayed them in the three wheeler having numerous mechanical problems.

For 1937, the Donington circuit had been especially lengthened for the RAC Tourist Trophy Race. The Tourist Trophy was the oldest engine race on record at that time, and still is. It was initially run on the Isle of Man in 1905 and moved to Northern Ireland, east of Belfast in 1928, when races were conducted on the Ards course. When the Ards layout was banned because of its deteriorating and dangerous driving condition, the Donington site was selected to stage the 1937-38 TT. The Donington Park modifications included a loop to eliminate Starkey's Corner which ran to the new Melbourne Corner, thereby lengthening the course from 2 miles 971 yards to 3 miles 220 yards.

On March 29, 1937, Donington Park again beckoned Henry and Red for the Easter Monday event. The 1084 bronze cased JTOR JAP and the Zoller were installed with 26 and 33 toothed sprockets for its chain drive. Running an Amal regulating the familiar 50/50 fuel mixture, the engine fired on Lodge BR 52 and 54 plugs. It was a fine day and Michael Faraday, Barbara's brother, filled the passenger's duties.

During practice the supercharger's blades tightened up so it was stripped down and reassembled with greater clearances and then worked satisfactorily. With a 40 second late start, Red ripped through the field, picked up time and overtook everyone except Taylor's Norton. Henry and Michael had to settle for second place with a speed of 58.37 mph.

Pushing Red around McLean's Bend at Donington, March 29, 1937

The Wye Valley Trial was held on April 3, 1937 and Yellow was ready for some exercise. So was Barbara, providing her acrobatic assistance over the tail of the trike as so many of the event's spectators had come to expect. It wasn't an easy day and the Lairds struggled to gain a second class award.

The Whit Monday meeting

Donington Park

Circuit from late 1937 through 1939 - 3 miles 220 yards

took place at Donington on May 17, 1937. Red was set up as for the earlier March event and Michael Faraday again passengered. Hale and Bate, driving other Morgans received a 30 second head start. Laird gave a 40 second head start to the motorcycles. Red ran really well for the first four laps. At the end of the fifth lap they had to pull out after some bolts sheared on the magneto platform. Laird still established a new one lap record for three wheelers at 61.20 mph. Hale managed to finish the race, placing third. Bate was less fortunate when he lost power at Starkey's Corner and retired.

Yellow was pressed back into action for the International Six Days' Trial in July at Llandrindod Wells in Wales. The Lairds ran the 1096 JAP without the Zoller this time and were successful in winning a Gold Medal.

The Bank Holiday Meeting at Donington August 2, 1937 was considered by many of the spectators to be the finest to date. Lovely, sunny weather, the largest entry to date and superb organization made an exciting event. The program listed four morning races in the 250, 350, 500 and 1100 cc classes, and the same classes in the afternoon, but under the category of Grand Prix classes for prize money. H.L. Daniell, astride his 348 Norton, broke the 350 cc record for 20 laps at 66.59 mph. He

The bridge over Starkey's Straight at Donington, Easter 1937. Note the mashall on the left

Celebrating the gold award for the ISDT at Llandrindod Wells in Wales, July 1937

Laird passing Cyril Hale in Number 95 at Starkey's Corner, August 2, 1937

The R.A.C. Tourist Trophy Race, September 4, 1937. The Laird crew are wearing armbands. Jim Goodall is on the far right

then went on to break the 500 cc record for the same distance at 67.68 mph.

Henry, passengered by Rodney Bainbridge, had Red out for some fun. In the five lap sidecar and three wheeler event, there were 6 sidecar outfits and 4 trikes in this impressive start. Red's engine was misfiring and they were last off the line, but some magnificent driving saw them roar through the field with such great effect that they finished in second place. L.W. Taylor also drove a great race in his sidecar outfit, took the lead in the second lap and held it to the end. W. Bibby, on his 596 Norton sidecar, attempted to pass Laird on the last lap at Starkey's Corner. Bibby brushed Laird slightly and did a complete somersault. Fortunately, there were no serious injuries and Laird continued.

L.W. Taylor's 596 Norton finished first with the time of 13 min 15.2 sec at 57.75 mph. Laird's second place time was 13 min 34.5 sec at 56.38 mph. Third through fifth places were taken by W.E. Bury's 746 Douglas, C. Hale's 990 Morgan, and V.S. Graham's 495 Grindlay-JAP.

The afternoon races witnessed thrills and spills in all classes, but none more exciting than in the 10 lap three wheeler and sidecar grand prix event. Seven sidecar entries and one Morgan comprised the field. Laird and Red were the last to start, but took the lead within a lap! They held this position for seven laps, hotly pursued by W.E. Bury's 746 Douglas in second, and L.W. Taylor's 596 Norton in third. Red went deathly silent on lap 7 and coasted onto the grass. Victory was lost when the engine began to seize after an oil pipe broke. Taylor passed Bury and took first place with a speed of 57.74 mph. Behind Taylor were Bury, Horton and Graham in that order.

Henry was back at Donington on September 4, 1937, but not in a three wheeler. He entered the RAC Tourist Trophy Race of 100 laps on the new course which measured 3 miles 220 yards. Driving the Morgan 4/4, his pit personnel were Barbara Laird, J. Woodhouse, George Goodall, Jim Goodall, *Fatty* Curtis and H.F.S. Morgan. All were hoping the Morgan could cover the 312 mile distance. A crowd estimated at 30,000 were there to enjoy the spectacle on this fine, hot day. Cars were restricted from parking near the railings, the few yards of separation giving the spectators room to move around for better views.

Twenty-nine entries made up a fine field with handicapping by credit laps and time. Charles Dodson's Austin, two time winner of the TT, was given 16 credit laps and 52 seconds over three Darracqs, Brackenbury & Martin's Lagonda and the Delahaye of Mognin & Paul.

At twelve noon the first to start were the three Singers and three Fiats running with 13 credit laps and a 2 min and 19 sec advantage. The Frazer Nash-BMWs from the German factory followed. Four BMWs were on the line, but the one driven by Dobbs snapped something in the rear axle area and was pushed off into the pits. A.C. Bertelli, the ex-employee from Aston Martin, headed up the German mechanics. Furious work commenced in dismantling the differential as the team had been committed to finish the race at all costs.

The first half of the race saw a duel between the Franco-German contingency with the Darracq in second place followed by the Frazer Nash-BMWs. Fane, one of the BMW drivers, lead the race on handicap in the early stages. Sommer, in his Darracq, went all out to pass Fane, driving at 130 mph on the downhill approach to Melbourne Corner. Just as it appeared he would be successful, his engine developed a terrible clatter as an exhaust valve broke off into the cylinder head. This let Comotti in his Darracq take up the lead position, maintaining the French honor. In 45 minutes he had secured the handicap lead from Fane.

The leading British car, Maclure's Riley, successfully passed Aldington's BMW to get into fifth place. His efforts were short lived, as valve problems stopped him.

Just after one o'clock, Comotti had to pull in for water and his teammate, LeBegue, took over the lead. The skill of the Darracq drivers was fascinating to watch as they replaced each other in the lead, waiting to move forward if there was trouble. At 1:15 PM the handicap order read: 1st – R. LeBegue (Darracq – 68.6 mph). 2nd – A.P.F. Fane (Frazer Nash-BMW). 3rd – G. Comotti (Darracq). 4th – B. Bira (Frazer Nash-BMW). 5th – H.J. Aldington (Frazer Nash-BMW). 6th – J. Paul (Delahaye).

Although many cars slid through Melbourne Corner, the Darracqs and BMWs appeared rock steady. Dobbs was still watching the German mechanics in the pits trying to get the splines loosened on one of the axle shafts on his BMW and it had now taken an hour and 45 minutes. He put on his gloves and helmet. Another 30 minutes would pass before the work was completed. Finally, after 2 hours and 15 minutes had passed, Dobbs received the applause of the crowd as he rejoined the race.

The cars continued to provide excitement all around the course as they drifted and screeched tires. The Laird's Morgan skidded onto the grass at Melbourne Corner. Paul's Delahaye did the same thing, but continued on without stopping. Comotti took a nasty skid at Holly Wood.

Fane came into the pits, but when he restarted the back axle made a crunching noise. The Germany mechanics had just previously finished with Dobb's car, but again got out the jacks. All to no avail, as it was obvious that Fane was finished, ending his brilliant attempt.

The Comotti's Darracq was still leading at 69.2 mph, closely followed by LeBegue in the Darracq, B. Bira in the Frazer Nash-BMW, Paul & Mognin's Delahaye, the Barne's Singer, and Dobson's Riley. The Dobson's Riley had been into the pits several times for brake adjustments, and twice for water, putting him way back in the running.

By 3:15 Aldington's Frazer Nash-BMW had taken sixth place behind the Singer and the Delahaye driven by Mognin, who seemed to be having one adventure after another. He skidded wildly several places, keeping the spectators alert. When he drove into the pits to have the brakes cooled, the water poured over them created a huge cloud of steam.

The Black's Singer moved into sixth place when Aldington's Frazer Nash-BMW began misfiring, and he came into the pits to have the plugs and jets cleaned. Now it was 3:45 PM and until the finish of the race the six leaders on handicap held their places. Aldington got back into the race, driving faster than ever. Dobbs, on the other hand, had more transmission problems and had to quit.

Earlier in the race, LeBegue had attained a speed of 72.6 mph with a lap of 2 min 35 seconds. Comotti ran his 98th lap at 73.5 mph in 2 min 33 sec, the fastest of the race.

During the final stages, two mishaps occurred which could have spelled disaster. The Blackbury & Martin Lagonda lost a wheel at the Hairpin. The Laird's Morgan broke a stub axle on the straight between Red Gate Corner and Holly Wood while traveling at 80 mph just after 4:18 PM. The left front wheel sailed off the car into the grass. Some really expert driving by Henry Laird saved both car and driver from disaster. The 4/4 was admired throughout the race for its steadiness and for its *on rail* cornering ability. It was hailed as a car which the consumer could buy as represented. The Morgan covered a total of 84 laps.

The Gordini's Fiat ran out of petrol on lap 99 and the

September 1937, Henry and Richard push Red after it quit during the race

driver ran to the pits from Melbourne Corner, returned with a gas can and finished within the time limit. Shapley, driving Dobson's Fiat, was one lap short of finishing when the race was called.

The results showed the Darracqs of Comotti and LeBegue running one-two at 68.7 and 67.5 mph respectively. Bira's Frazer Nash-BMW was in third at 66.1 mph followed by the Barnes' Singer at 57.8 mph. In fifth place was the Paul & Mognin Delahaye at 65.9 mph. Running in sixth was N. Black's Singer at 56.3 mph. No team finished the race due to darkness.

Barbara Laird recorded times for the Morgan 4/4 on laps 6 through 84. Included were two pit stops. The first took 59.6 sec for 5 gallons of petrol and a look at the oil and water levels. The second pit stop ran 1 min 52 sec for water and a brake adjustment. The Coventry Climax engine was using a Solex carburetor and KLG plugs.

An available chart converted minutes and seconds to miles per hour. On lap 58 with a time of 3 min. 10 sec. the speed would equal 59.2 mph. This seemed to be the Morgan's best time. The slowest time was on lap 6 with 3 min. 28 sec. for 54.1 mph. All of the times were at the 3 minute mark with the difference ranging between 11 and 18 seconds. That averages between 56.8 and 59.2 miles per hour. Not bad for a Morgan 4/4 running on Donington Park's twisty circuit.

Henry Laird took Red back to Brooklands on September 11, 1937 for the Hutchinson 100, a distance of 37 laps of the outer circuit. Before the actual 100 got underway, two events were run on the Mountain Circuit and two circuit handicaps were run on the main track. While these races were being conducted, most of the entrants for the main event were spending time warming up their motors and fending off the strong, biting cold wind. A variety of covers were thrown over the motors to conserve their heat.

Henry, whose passenger was Bill Clarke (of HRD Vincent fame), had Red set up the same as in his last race in 1936. Of the 33 entrants, they were the only representatives of the passenger class for this handicap event, open to solos, sidecars, and three wheelers.

An allotment of one minute in the pits was allowed for competitors to refuel. Only two people chose to pass on this allocation. The event began at 4:15 PM and 14 minutes elapsed before the last entrant left the start line. It wasn't long before the first trouble began when O.E. deLissa on a 348 Velocette stopped on the second lap to change a plug. The Laird's Morgan would not start at all for several minutes, and when it finally did, had to pull into the pits after one lap to change plugs. Other misfiring problems occurred with the 499 Vincent HRD ridden by G.E. Gott.

After several laps, Jock West on his 346 AJS still ran well and approached nearly 95 mph, although after 10 laps remained among the back markers. Ron Harris, astride a 490 Norton, lapped at over 100 mph and looked to be a serious contender for first place although he had a large handicap to overcome.

At the end of 10 laps the leaders were T.L. Beamish on a 246 New Imperial, W.R. Lunn on his 348 Velocette and in third, G.J. Burrell on a 490 Norton. The number of drop outs increased rapidly. B.L. Marsh on his 346 Excelsior retired with carburetion problems. E.J. Tubb seized the engine on his Grindlay Peerless. O.E. deLissa's Velocette was pulled in on the end of a tow rope. N. Cox on his 348 Norton also had to withdraw with a split silencer.

Henry Laird, who was lapping between 85 and 90 mph, continued to have plug misfiring due to a faulty magneto. He struggled to complete 11 laps but had to retire. After changing plugs before lap one began, he ran that lap in 2 min. 40 4/5 sec. For lap 4 he posted a time of 1 min. 55 sec. Lap 10 was covered in 1 min. 51 4/5 sec., but by lap 11 he had slowed all the way back to 2 min. 15 sec.

There were still lessons to be learned when it came to racing and Henry Laird and Red seemed to be weathering these together. Henry had already achieved a respected status as a competitor with his racer, Red. Would the racing trike survive to continue its heritage?

The War Years and Beyond, 1938-60

In 1938, the TT, sponsored by the RAC, again selected Donington Park, even though some people thought a better road circuit was deserving for a race of this rank. Donington Park, however, was recognized to be the best available at the moment. Several changes took place for this year's event with five scratch races scheduled and the Tourist Trophy going to the best on handicap. The RAC ruled that prototype cars could be entered, probably to bolster the flagging interest in the TT race. However, the Morgan and Aston Martin car firms still gave their support. Cars competed in five capacity classes which conformed to International Standards. Vehicles also had to carry mudguards and touring equipment.

The 1938 R.A.C. Rally. Barbara Laird chatting with George Goodall

The 1098 cc Morgan 4/4 was Henry's entry in the Donington Park Tourist Trophy Race, run over the 3.5 mile course as in 1937. The course had been described as very difficult and also very interesting by Rene LeBegue, who had taken second in a Darracq the previous year. Cars competed in classes comprised of 750 to 1100 cc, 1101 to 1500 cc, 1501 to 2000 cc, 2001 to 3000 cc and 3001 to 5000 cc. The largest engine cars had to start at scratch with those of a smaller capacity given credit laps ranging from 2 to 13 laps.

Entered in the smallest class were the Morgan 4/4, two Simca Fiats, a Fiat Balilla, a Riley, a 1087 cc MG, three Singer Nines and a 936 cc MG. The 1.5 litre class had two HRGs, three Rileys, a Triumph and two Lancias. Following this, the 2 liter class saw six 328 Frazer Nash-BMWs, four of which were *works* cars in the hands of H.J. Aldington, A.P.F. Fane, Bira and Dick Seaman, whom Mercedes-Benz had released to drive. A solitary Aston Martin had formidable foes to race. The only 3 litre entry was Louis Gerard from France with a blue 2988 cc Delage. Four 4.5 litre works Darracqs were the largest cars entered and ran against a 3.3 Bugatti driven by T.A.S.O. Mathieson.

The pack roared off the starting line at noon under gray skies, but on a dry roadbed. The large Darracqs pulled out in front with the 3 litre Delage close behind. The Bugatti tried to escape Fane's Frazer Nash-BMW, which was right on its tail. Dick Seaman acted as pace maker for the BMWs, which interested the British spectators. But the BMW cars began having trouble as Fane came in with a loose cover and Bira stripped his second gear.

The Delage, which Gerard was driving, did some 360-degree spins as the road became wet; but he drove with aggressive abandon and held the lead on handicap several hours into the event, averaging 69.92 mph. The two *works* Darracqs were even faster at 70 mph leading Lace's Delage. The Aston Martin, handled impressively by Seaman, was just behind in fifth position.

In the finale, it was the Delage which came in first in 4 hours 31 min. 50 sec. at 67.61 mph. The pushrod Aston Martin followed in 4 hours 35 min. 2 sec. at 65.45 mph. Following were the three Darracqs, a Singer, Riley, Simca-Fiat and a Singer running eighth, right on down to 24th position which Henry Laird held with the Morgan, completing 93 laps at 52.78 mph. Throughout the race there were no accidents and only five cars retired. Twenty-six cars finished with the fastest lap run at 72.6 mph by Carriere in one of the 4.5 litre *works* Darracqs.

This was Henry's last race. He accepted a position as Midlands Editor for *Motor Cycling* magazine under the editorship of Graham Walker. Because employment rules forbade competition work, Henry would never again race his two beloved Morgans, Red and Yellow, but he didn't turn his back on Morgans. The fact that he knew so much about them would soon manifest itself in his writings.

An example of his penmanship appeared in the January 4, 1940 issue of *Motor Cycling* magazine. In this article, he covered the subject of the Morgan suspension, expressing an appreciation with some practical suggestions. Using drawings of the 2-speeder M-chassis, he illustrated and discussed the installation of the double disc Andre shock absorber over the rear wheel on Red, his racer. *Uncle* George Goodall was credited with the actual fitting, carried out in the following manner. "Two pivot pins were fixed in the ends of a tubular bridge, which passed over the top of the wheel. The pins were free to rock in two bushed holes machined in the original fork blades. The top of the bridge had provision for a Silent bloc bush belonging to one arm of the shock absorber, the other arm being bolted to a bracket attached above the bevel box top. This decreased the clearance between the wheel and the body, so a hump was made and covered with canvas which permitted the necessary movement without anything hitting the body."

Henry continued, saying that when he had Red out for his first LCC Race at Brooklands, lapping at around 100 mph, the Morgan's stability was really proven. However, even with improved shocks, the bumps at Brooklands still created a jolting ride. He thought enough of the rear wheel shock absorber idea to try it on Yellow. When Red was converted from a two-speeder to a gearbox drive the rear shock and fork assembly was transferred to Yellow just prior to the ISDT in 1935. Henry devised a new system for Red.

He went to a breaker's yard and, for the princely sum of less than two shillings, obtained two Hartford shocks. These shocks were mounted on either side of the rear wheel on pivots made with pins and plates, mounted over the forks. This system allowed the forks and shocks to pivot freely. Brackets were fabricated to mount on top of the leaf springs which anchored the front of the shocks to the chassis cross brace which also secured the gearbox.

Henry mentioned that he had traveled many thousands of miles in Morgans, with many of those on the Continent during competition work. He had no doubt that a shock absorber on the rear wheel was a great improvement under any conditions short of puttering around the countryside on a Sunday run with your Great Aunt!

His articles continued. In the June 6, 1940 issue of *Motor Cycling*, he related his knowledge about racing and trials, and offered practical tips to Morgan owners on how to apply his experiences.

He related how he had stayed at a hotel in Ambleside for a week while indulging in one of his favorite pursuits, fell walking and climbing. He used the trusty side valve Morgan on this trip. While standing outside one evening, he and his brother, Richard, observed the performance of a Morgan JAP ohv model purring along before Kirkstone Pass. When the driver approached the grade of 1 in 7, he simply opened up the throttle, still in third gear, and roared up the incline with lusty sounding exhausts. Boy! From that moment on, he had to have one of the new 10/40 hp overhead JAP Morgans. He figured that this acquisition would give him the edge and he could stage a good show against some of his friends who had 3-litre Bentleys and Grand Prix Austin Sevens. He soon proved that only the Bentley could beat him for outright speed. On top gear acceleration and for hill climbing, Henry declared, the Morgan was superior to all others. He described how his friends were envious of his new JAP model which only cost 150 Pounds against their outlay of from 185 to 1,125 Pounds for their cars; also stressing the advantage of licensing the Morgan for 5 Pounds annually, as opposed to sports cars which cost their owners 25s per horsepower to register. By special application, fuel was granted for the Morgan on the same basis as a four wheeler of the same RAC rated horsepower.

Henry was aware that, with the war raging, many people faced hardships including increased taxation, and stored their cars during the turmoil. Some people sold their vehicles or turned to motorcycle transport. Those who were used to motoring in two seater sports cars, didn't take kindly to dressing in the garb necessary for motorcycling. Besides, if a man had a wife or girl friend who was used to a car, he wouldn't expect her to ride on a motorcycle. Therefore, Henry declared it was only right and proper to turn one's attention to a Super Sports Morgan.

The uninitiated may have looked upon Morgans as being difficult, but Henry contended that three wheelers were much safer at speed than some so-called sports cars. Even though the steering seemed heavy, it could be handled and skids could be controlled before becoming dangerous.

Henry recommended a foot throttle to delete the hand throttle effort, making it easier to change gears, and to drive in general. In fact, Henry had one installed on Red for a time. He suggested that braking methods should be practiced, using the hand brake as much as possible to avoid locking up the rear wheel on tram lines or other slippery surfaces.

He addressed some reader's nervous questions about Morgans turning over. "They will turn over, but so will a four wheeler, if the driver makes it. I have been in some pretty tight corners on a trials model, and a racer, but only twice have I upended the trials model – once on Washgates and once outside Derby. On both occasions I was going much too fast under the prevailing circumstances and driving a machine with an 8-inch ground clearance instead of the Super Sports normal 4.5 inches."

The article went on to discuss the ownership of the two speed models and how to maintain the chassis, suspension, and mechanical aspects. It mentioned that the 1933 models had detachable and interchangeable wheels, a big improvement over the earlier models which had loose ball bearings and the cup and cone arrangement in the front hubs. "For 1933, the 60-degree 10-40 JAP motor had front crank starting, but beware if there was a backfire, as injury could result to the winder's hand and the motor's timing pinion. When the cone clutch was replaced by the single plate dry clutch, gear change problems cleared up. The Dunlop Magna spare wheel, mounted on top of the tail area, subtracted from the luggage carrying area, so it was usually removed."

Further along in the article, Laird discussed the positive points and the improvements made when the 50-degree ohv Matchless motors began appearing on new Morgan models in 1934. This was also the year the 8 hp four cylinder Ford motor was introduced with the motor mounted behind the radiator in enclosed fashion.

For the 1935 season, the Super Sports models had the V-twin Matchless motors. The water cooled example was preferred over the air cooled model, as the former was quieter and could go longer between periods of decarbonizing.

In 1936, the 10 hp Ford motor was presented and offered fine performance. In some respects, it was, perhaps, the most attractive proposition of the three speed models to an ex-car owner for various reasons. The article stated, "The motor is conventional in the eyes of the car world, also the oiling system, the starter motor and the electrical layout follow normal lines. The brakes are coupled to the pedal, whereas, in the past, the front brakes were operated by a central hand lever and the rear brake only by the pedal."

Girling brakes were fitted as standard to a new four cylinder Super Sports model in 1938. All three brakes were coupled to the pedal. "The body work of this new model resembles the front end of the Morgan 'Four-Four' and the rear end of the super three wheeler. A folding screen is standard, whilst a door enables the hood to remain erect whilst mounting or dismounting."

"The 1939 programme saw no change, but during that year Girling brakes were fitted to the V-twin super sports models, the front being operated by the pedal and the rear by a central hand-cum parking brake."

In closing the article, Henry Laird stated that he had endeavored to give a brief outline of the Morgans which should make a very strong appeal to the ex-sports car owners. "For those who can live without any unnecessary frills, and want optimum performance, some of the old 50-degree JAP motor two-speed machines are excellent conveyances. On the other hand, many car owners want self starters, coil ignition, a spare wheel and all the other paraphernalia which have become part and parcel of modern cars; this class is catered for by some of the later Super Sports twins and all the four-cylinder Supers. Whatever your choice, I only hope that any future Morgan driver will have as much fun and good service as I have had in the past from these wonderful little passenger machines."

Although Henry Laird's last motorsport event with either Red or Yellow was in September, 1937, he found another way to enjoy his interests by acting as passenger to George Brough in his Brough Superior sidecar. Henry and George got along famously. George always complimented and appreciated Henry's thoroughness. While in a pub with others during a trip through some sections in Derbyshire, Henry used to slip outside and check the tire pressures, making sure they were within a half pound of each other.

George entered the London-Edinburgh Trial on June 3, 1938 with his Brough sidecar outfit and asked Henry to passenger. Barbara Laird, not to be left out, passengered for A.G. Zug Sugden in his 1938 MX2 Super Sports beetle back, a three speed gearbox model, but fitted with two speed nondetachable front wheels.

When Henry joined the staff of *Motor Cycling*, the Morgans, Red and Yellow went to Tom Bryant of Parkstone for safe keeping. Tom was Joe Huxham's business partner at Bournemouth and they both agreed to give the two Morgans a good home.

Tom Bryant took Red to Donington Park on May 27, 1939. Making his debut with the racer, he entered it in the first 8 Lap Sidecar Race. The handicap system had finally been altered so that Morgans and 600 cc sidecars were on equal terms, starting on scratch. Running without the supercharger, Tom advanced to the second place spot by the second lap and held it to the end, having a good dice with A. Horton and Taylor, both on Nortons. Tom finished the race with a record speed of 62 mph.

The second sidecar race took place in the afternoon and Bryant had to give 64 seconds to Burke's 996 cc Morgan. Driving Red flat out, he could gain no ground on either Taylor's or Horton's Nortons, and spun out at Melbourne. This gave him a fourth place finish.

On August 5, 1939, Red and Bryant returned to Donington Park for more sidecar racing. He was still running without the supercharger, using twin Amals. In the first sidecar race he had a bad start, but managed to make up ground and passed Horton at the half way point. The competition gained momentum and both drivers gave it everything they had. Horton managed to pass Bryant again, but braked too late at Red Gate, and went off on the slip road. Tom Bryant went on to finish in second place with a speed average of 61.96 mph. In the second race for sidecars and three wheelers, Tom had braking problems and didn't place in the results.

In 1939 several important races were held at Donington. There was the British Empire Trophy Race on April 1, the Nuffield Trophy Race on June 10, a Cambridge UAC Meeting at the end of June, and a VSCC meet on August 12. This latter meeting in August proved to be the last meet for auto racing for some years.

The last meet for motorcycles took place on Saturday, August 26, 1939, just eight days before World War II broke out. It was an International Grand Prix event featuring a 20 lap race for 500 cc machines. A four cylinder blown works AJS ridden by Bob Foster was among the entrants. The winners of that final race were Freddie Frith on a Norton at 73.69 mph in 50 min. 53.4 sec. for the 62.5 miles. Second was Arthur Wellsted, also astride a Norton, and third went to Peter Goodman on a Velocette.

The third Donington Grand Prix, which had been scheduled for September 30, 1939, had to be abandoned, although the regulations had already been printed.

With the outbreak of war, Donington Park was requisitioned by the Military and developed into the largest Transport Base in England. During the war, the track deteriorated and tons of garbage piled up. It was as late as 1956 before all the debris was finally cleared away from the track and its derelict buildings.

In addition to Donington Park, other locations were affected. On August 7, 1939, with the clouds of war looming on the horizon, the BARC held a final meet which was the last opportunity to see racing at Brooklands. Two demonstration runs and twelve races were scheduled beginning at 1:00 PM with a large crowd in attendance. Racing that day featured MGs, ERAs, and others. Present also were some pre-1905 vintage autos and several early motoring tricycles.

Tom Bryant races Red at Donington Park, August 5, 1939

During the Second World War, Brooklands was again requisitioned as it had been in 1914. Aircraft had to be manufactured and tested so hangers were erected over the track's concrete. Workshops sprang up on the Railway Straight and portions of the track were broken up and removed. What a pity, but there was a war to be won!

Laird's friend, Arthur Maskell, who had arranged for Henry to buy Red, suffered real heartbreak in the bombing blitz on London in 1940 when his business "Maskell For Morgans" was destroyed. He retired to Tolworth, remaining there until his death in 1963.

Very tragically, Henry Laird was killed at age 33 in March 1941. He was riding a 350 Triumph motorcycle at night during a blackout period while returning to Home Guard Duty. A lorry pulled out in front of him and his motorcycle struck it broadside with fatal results.

The years of World War II (1939-1945) affected the production of Morgans at the factory, as well as calling a halt to road racing for those years; but positive enthusiasm for the cycle cars remained high. Dennis Griffin promoted his idea of forming a club for owners of Morgan three wheelers by writing to Trepenpol in *Motor Cycling* magazine in 1944. This laid the ground work for the formation of the Morgan Three Wheeler Club. In September 1945, an inaugural meeting was conducted at the Morgan Factory and over 50 enthusiasts attended.

In December 1945, the Morgan Factory announced their new three wheeler models. The F4 four seater Ford engine models and the F-Super two seater models were the only trikes on the assembly lines. Sadly, no twins were offered. A batch of 12 Matchless twins were assembled from left over chassis and motors and nine of these MX4 Super Sports were dispatched to Brylaws of Melbourne, Australia in 1946. Some of them still survive.

Racing returned to post-War England but not to Brooklands. At the end of the War, for reasons not entirely clear, the track was sold to Vickers-Armstrong, Ltd. for 330,000 Pounds Sterling. Vickers was absorbed into the British Aircraft Corporation until 1974 when a large part of Brooklands was sold to Oyster Lane Properties, Ltd. With all of the construction that had taken place, it was surprising that 90% of the original track and buildings remained.

Other tracks throughout England were created on country estates or abandoned runways. Cadwell Park, Brough Aerodrome, Queensferry, Ansty Aerodrome, Haddenham Aerodrome, Silverstone and Thruxton Aerodrome provided a variety of tracks and circuits for racing enthusiasts.

Barbara Laird married a close family friend, Freddy Clark, in December, 1946. Clark was the Experimental Department Chief for Triumph in Coventry. Barbara never had any children, saying, "Morgans were my children." Another tragedy hit Barbara when Freddy died on September 14, 1947.

Barbara Laird offered "one of her children," Henry's Red, to C.E. Titch Allen in 1948 for the sum of £100. The offer was refused due to storage complications and because the racer had such limited usage. Red was not suitable as a family vehicle, and there was no provision for starting aside from hand pushing. It remained in the hands of Tom Bryant at Huxhams Ltd. in Parkstone, Dorset.

One unlikely site for road races was the layout at Blandford Army Camp in Dorset. Tom Bryant took Red out of storage and entered the sidecar races on September 3, 1949. Red suffered mechanical problems and they retired early in the day.

Blandford Army Camp was the location again on April 29, 1950 for an Auto Cycle Union (ACU) international race. Tom entered Red, still running on twin Amals, as in its pre-war events. Red began in last

Tom Bryant poses with Red at Blandford Farm, April 29, 1950

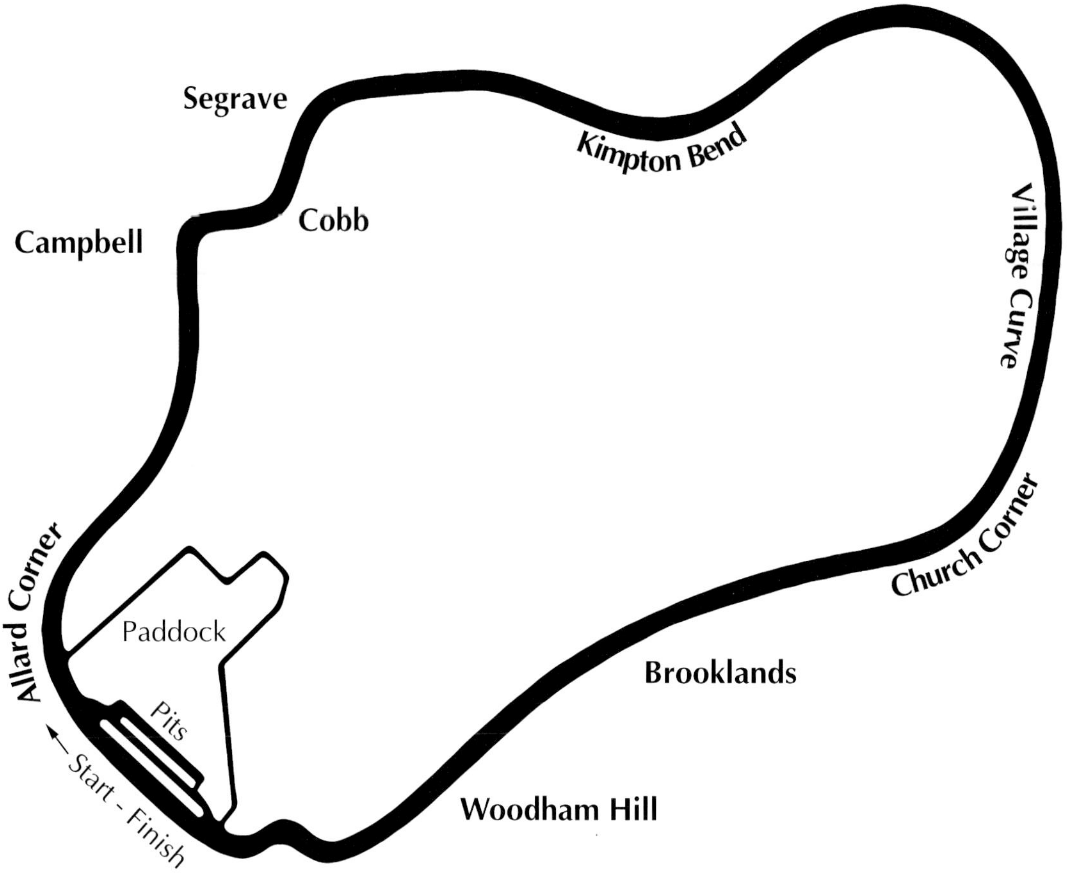

Thruxton Circuit
2.356 miles

spot in a three row grid but advanced through the field whipping the Norton bikes of Taylor and Smith and taking a first place with a speed of 67.7 mph.

Petrol rationing remained in effect following the war, and participants in contests of speed had to guard those valuable petrol coupons. Rationing finally ended in June 1950.

Tom Bryant, still enjoying Red, entered it on August 6, 1951 for the ACU International Road Race at Thruxton. Tom and Red took second after Cyril Smith's Norton's first place in the 8 lap passenger event. This was the last race in which Red would participate for many years, although Tom did take it out in 1954 for an appearance at Silverstone for Motor Cycling Day .

Tom Bryant races Red at Blandford Farm, April 29, 1950

In early 1955, the editor of the MTWC's monthly *The Bulletin*, Harry Latham, and his friend, Eddie Moore, paid a visit to Huxhams. They enjoyed a chat with Tom Bryant about the history of Red and took some photos. Tom stated that Red was for sale to anyone with a genuine interest in racing it. The 1084 cc bronze crankcase JAP with the Baronia bronze heads, twin racing Amals, Bosch magneto, and fair tires were still in place. In fact, it was ready to be raced on the first track in sight!

Word circulated about Red's availability and Hugh Dyer, an interior decorator from Sussex, became interested. In a note to Tom Bryant on March 7, 1955, he mentioned a reference he had seen about it in *The Bulletin*. Tom sent back a letter stating some of Red's history, offering it for the amount of 160 Pounds. Dyer wrote back on March 17 saying he was able to raise the money. Bryant penned another letter on March 19 stating he hoped Hugh would come along and see the trike as there were two other interested parties wishing to buy it. Shortly after that, Hugh Dyer made final arrangements and secured the racer.

Hugh corresponded with Tom in November, 1956 sending some photos of Red now fitted with lights and the number plate KDY 78. Hugh stated that the motor had a cracked cam follower and was experiencing clutch vibration. His installation of a 6-volt starter was not working. Tom suggested he use a 12-volt battery. They discussed brakes which Tom conceded were never very good and suggested a conversion to hydraulics on the front.

During the next four years at some point, Hugh Dyer got over zealous in his driving, exceeded in over revving the engine, and threw a rod which wedged between the bronze crankcases. Many years later, Tom Bryant admitted that while Red was stored during the war, the Castrol R wasn't drained out of the bronze cases causing them to somewhat decompose. The long storage also wasn't kind to the rods and bearings.

Following the blown-up engine incident, the trike came into the possession of John H. Staveley and George Oliver at Mercury Motors in Middlesex. They scrambled and located a JAP Brough Superior KTOR sprint engine. This was the 8/45 50-degree air cooled twin. The timing chest was stamped with KTOR/T 49039. This replacement engine was fitted to Red and it was again looking for a buyer.

A long journey lay ahead for Red, with a trip across the Atlantic to America. It would be quite a few years before anyone would again see the Red racer on the track.

When peace finally returned, ending World War II, Yellow was sold to a member of the Vintage MCC who desired it for his teenage son. The youngster operated it with a motorcycle license. It next passed to David Baxter, a Farnborough Apprentice in the RAF, who was looking for *cheap transport*. After that, it dropped out of sight.

Several years later, it was spotted in a London garage in a run down condition. C.E. Titch Allen heard about it and contacted the owner who was surprised to learn about its trials history. Titch offered to buy Yellow, but the owner refused figuring it was worth some money and had increased in value since he discovered its history. He drove it for a while and then blew up the engine, damaging the connecting rods. It was too much for him to repair.

In 1960, the owner offered to sell it to Titch who quickly seized the opportunity despite the needed repairs. Since Titch owned a set of rods and flywheels out of a 1150 Brough, he was able to make the engine repairs. Yellow had been painted green prior to when Titch acquired it and he wanted to return it to the original primrose color as when it was used in trials by the Lairds. He visited Barbara Laird and asked her to select the correct color. This was difficult with so many shades of yellow paint from which to choose, but she finally produced a hank of wool of the correct shade. Titch had Mason's Paints, a firm in Derby, mix a color to match the wool and Yellow was repainted. Since that time Titch has kept Yellow in its 1930s trials condition and it still has the 1098 cc water cooled JAP which was swapped back and forth between it and Red. Yellow resides in the Stanford Hall Motorcycle Museum, when not used for Morgan or motorcycle outings and special events.

Clive Lones' racer and the Tommy Rhodes' trike which, along with Henry Laird's Red, comprised the Morgan Factory Team entries in the 1933-35 LCC Relay Races at Brooklands both survive, as well.

The Clive Lones' trike was mentioned in 1949 in an article in *Motor Cycling* where it appeared in a photo with the registration number EGK 505. John Lindop of Chester tracked it down in 1954 in Derby and purchased it. The original LTOW engine had gone to the scrap heap because parts couldn't be found. A JAP JTO twin replaced it. Lindop used it, not in racing, but for personal speed enjoyment. He experimented with various fuels, alcohol and petrol-benzole mixtures, and blew up the engine twice. He finally got it running satisfactorily and did some restoration on the body. In 1960 he ran an ad in the Morgan Club's magazine *The Bulletin*, advertising it as a 1929 two speed Brooklands Morgan which held 36 world records. It was advertised in concours condition for a price of 180 Pounds Sterling. Alan Goldsmith purchased it and kept it in his garage near London for a number of years. He passed away at age 87 on June 27, 1992. The trike then went to Jerry Larke, who has preserved it as a period racer, so far resisting the temptation to use it in speed events.

Clive Lones, who attained so many records with his three wheeler, didn't retire from racing until the 1960s. He stayed in touch with the Morgan movement and attended some Morgan events and an

Annual Group Meeting of the MTWC. He lived until November 1981 when he finally succumbed after bravely fighting a long illness.

The Tommy Rhodes' racer, YY 49, was stored in a corner of the Portus and Rhodes Garage until purchased by Gordon King in 1949. Gordon used it in sprints and had some success. He removed the original body so he could use one made of fiberglass in an attempt to reduce the trike's weight. King advertised it in an issue of *The Bulletin* in 1954 after it had been fitted with a new big end assembly. It was painted green, fully road equipped and available for a reasonable offer.

Morgan enthusiast Bill Wallbank obtained it in 1955 and spent over two years locating the correct parts and restoring it to the racing look it had in the 1930s at Brooklands. Bill used it on many occasions for racing, even taking it to Germany for several events at the Nurburgring in 1979 and 1980. Today it still gets used, and Bill made an appearance with it at the 50th Anniversary of the founding of the MTWC in Great Malvern in 1995.

Red's American Adventures, 1961-90

Mercury Motors advertised Red in several publications, one of these catching the attention of Paul Moyer in Marblehead, Massachusetts. Paul made a deposit on the trike, but was lax in making final arrangements for shipping. In a letter from Mercury Motors dated September 7, 1961, the firm inquired why Paul hadn't responded to their letter of May 5. The Morgan was taking up valuable space on their premises and they wanted it moved. The following month Red was shipped out of England and arrived in America in October, 1961. The shipment included the damaged bronze engine cases, the Baronia bronze heads, and the Zoller supercharger.

Red in Marblehead, MA when Vic Hyde acquired it in 1967

When Moyer unpacked Red, he expected it to be ready to jump in and drive away. Instead, he found that it needed a chain, sprockets, and other items. Red was actually in very rough condition, so Moyer began taking it apart for restoration. He stored Red's pieces in an old shed behind a rental house he owned. Gradually, the trike became covered with his excess personal furniture. Red's restoration was put on hold while Moyer continued his French studies in Paris as part of his school teaching. He also spent time with another of his interests, yachting. In addition, he had announced plans to be married. Red was still competing for Moyer's attention but it placed very low on his list of priorities.

The rumor of an old Morgan three wheeler lying in a shed in New England found its way to a special individual who had a passion for three wheelers of every description. This was Vic Hyde, the traveling musician and one man band, the Honorary Mayor of Niles, Michigan. Vic got in touch with Paul Moyer, but was told the Morgan was not for sale. Paul wouldn't even allow Vic to view it. Vic asked that Paul let him know if he should change his mind. Vic would occasionally drop Paul a postcard describing his musical travels, subtly keeping his option open.

Vic Hyde was an international musical phenomenon, playing his music from multiple horns and key boards. He performed at fairs and grand openings, on cruise ships, in palladiums and Las Vegas. He was the Master of Ceremonies for stars such as Crystal Gayle, Sonny James and others. A book could be written about his musical career and his car collecting. On many of his trips around the country he would trailer one or more of his unusual three wheeled autos and display them, either where he was performing, or nearby in a storefront or other building so the public could admire his unusual tricars and his restoration work. The inventory of autos in Vic's three wheeler collection prior to June 1977, comprised 3 Bonds, 3 Messerschmidts, a Spatz, 2 Berkeleys, 6 Morgans, a Davis, a Noble and 2 Reliants. Thirty-three vehicles total, mostly with three wheels. By the end of 1977 he had 39 three wheelers in his collection. At one time he was associated with the Rolls Royce Owners Club, and over the years had owned 7 of that make. What a character; he lived for his music and his cars!

Two years passed since Vic first heard of Paul Moyer's Morgan in Massachusetts. Then one day out of the blue he received a phone call from Paul saying that the old shed where the Morgan was stored was being razed. Would Vic still be interested in purchasing the trike? Paul told Vic that he had first crack at it since no one else had expressed any interest. Paul offered it to Vic for $550, the amount he had invested. Vic's excitement knew no bounds, but he had to wait for two days while he completed a musical engagement. As soon as the gig ended, he hitched a trailer to his Rolls Royce and drove the 1,000 miles to collect the Morgan.

The JAP KTOR Sprint engine acquired with Red in 1967

The sloping fuel tank was designed to fit under the reshaped cowling installed in 1936

When he arrived at Moyer's place, he found the trike in a derelict condition, the engine, body and chassis in separate pieces. Bearings and various engine components were lying in the dirt on the floor of the old shed. After almost four hours, Vic had the Morgan assembled enough to roll it onto his trailer. Vic scrounged the premises for remaining parts and packed them into the trunk of the Rolls for safe transport. These items included the Zoller supercharger, the damaged bronze engine cases, and the Baronia bronze cylinder heads. An old photo album showing Red racing in the 1930s had been assembled by John Lindop and this was added to the cache.

Paul mentioned that during the time he owned the trike he had driven it about four miles and he felt a rod might have bent. Vic, with his inherent knowledge about Morgan trikes, interpreted this to mean the exterior flywheel had slipped. This proved to be the case.

When able to examine the old Morgan more closely at home, Vic noted its sloping cowl, and recalled reading a particular article in one of his back issues of *Motor Sport*. The article mentioned a car called Yellow and another one with a sloping front cowl which was used for racing. Was this Red? Could this be the same trike in the article that he now owned? Vic contacted several members of the Morgan Three Wheeler Club in England by letter. He sent over numbers from the gearbox and engine. No chassis number was found. A short time later he received confirmation that he had purchased Henry Laird's famous Red racing Morgan! The purchase had taken place on June 15, 1967.

In England during 1967, other developments took place. A small group of enthusiasts interested in preserving the Brooklands track, buildings, and associated grounds, formed the Brooklands Society, Ltd. The Society was instrumental in having some areas preserved and in opening a Brooklands Museum for the public's enjoyment.

Back in the States, Vic took time out of his busy work schedule to enjoy his love of three wheelers. On June 27, 1970 he jumped in his 1952 Morgan F-Super, traveled to Colorado, and ascended Pike's Peak. This feat took him nearly 4 hours because he had to stop numerous times to refill the radiator and let the engine cool. The engine quit 8 times with overheating and vapor lock before he finally completed the 19 mile journey ascending the peak to an elevation of 14,100 feet. As far as can be ascertained, this is the one and only time that a Morgan three wheeler has made the ascent to the top of Pike's Peak.

Other events were taking place in England during

Red's neglected chassis showing the front cable braking system

Original plate used when towing Red to the races

this time with the racing scene. Donington Park had not been used for racing since the outbreak of World War II. In September 1971, wealthy real estate owner and land developer, Bernard Tom Wheatcroft, purchased the track along with 300 additional acres of park land. His dream was to return racing to the area. Before that could happen many obstacles had to be overcome including a lot of work to the track.

Shortly after his acquisition of Red, Vic Hyde heard that Barbara Laird, now Barbara Laird Drummond, owned some literature and items that would complete Red's history by adding to the Lindop photo album. He wrote to Barbara on May 11, 1968 and inquired about these items. The paraphernalia included the original English Log Book, the front YY 19 number plate, four period photos in black frames, the original lap racing charts she recorded on lined note paper, and very importantly, the Brooklands Gold Star.

While Donington Park was being renovated, Vic went back to the U.K. in 1972 on another musical engagement and three wheeler buying escapade. During his trip he met Barbara Laird Drummond. Barbara lost her husband, Captain Drummond, RN in 1970. She was planning on leaving her present home in May 1972, so Vic's timing was good. Vic and Barbara visited. At first, she was of a mind to keep the historical items relating to Red and its racing history as mementos, but she finally agreed to sell them. They agreed on a price of 100 Pounds for everything. He left a 20 Pound note as deposit, promising to send the balance when he returned home to Michigan.

On a subsequent trip to England, Vic was a house guest of Clarrie Coombes and somehow misplaced the Gold Star while he was showing it off. Clarrie and Vic later said the Gold Star turned up in Clarrie's vacuum cleaner when the guest room was cleaned. Clarrie kept the treasured Gold Star for several weeks, showing it around to Morgan Club Members and then mailed it back to Vic in Niles, Michigan.

The next chapter in the life of Red began with Hyde's restoration. He separated the chassis from the body and found the original wooden body frame in excellent condition. The KTOR 50-degree JAP engine was delivered to Fred Booth for an overhaul. Meanwhile, Vic filled dozens of holes in the body's sheet metal using a torch and coat hangers for filler. Apparently many modifications had been tried over the years resulting in those holes. He invested countless hours using polyester body filler to smooth its wavy surface.

The old aluminum facia panel was replaced, but the original wood retained. New wind scallops were fabricated because the old ones had been lost. The beetle back skirt originally had six vertical louvers. One of these had been welded shut at some point when Red was still in England. Vic left it in that configuration. He spent hours straightening the other battered louvers.

He converted the front brakes to hydraulics, but wasn't pleased with the job. Apparently, the master cylinder was too large and caused problems.

With little work remaining, the body frame and panels were nearly ready for painting. Vic transported them to a local body shop in Niles for final preparation and paint. He then left for England on another trip. Upon his return, he went to the body shop to collect Red's body but was shocked instead when he found the place boarded up and gutted to the walls. No sign of the owner could be found. Vic was in a panic! He made inquiries all around town. Two months later, a tip led to a farm field. There, he found Red's body panels being engulfed by weeds. Surprisingly, they had survived with no dents and only slight surface rust. Collecting them, he returned everything to his garage and promised himself not to leave Red unattended in the future. He personally completed the preparation work for painting.

A short time later, Vic entertained at a banquet in Niles for the local Soap Box Derby sponsored by the local Chevrolet dealer. In exchange for his time, Vic was promised a paint job for Red. The color chosen was 1969 Corvette Red lacquer.

After being painted, the body was bolted onto the chassis which Vic had painted white. The woodwork was gray. Vic thought the trike looked pretty good at this point. He retrieved the engine from Fred Booth and installed it on the chassis. With enthusiasm bubbling over, he drove Red about five miles before the external flywheel shifted. What a let down. He had put in so much work to get things to this point. Vic had been unaware Fred hadn't tightened the securing main shaft nut. The engine was again pulled off, and this time, taken to Tom Pelletiere, who Vic knew did motorcycle restoration and engine work. Tom was asked to correct the problem and check over Fred's work.

Red's body frame and skirt were found in a field near Niles, Michigan

The body frame and skirt fitted in Vic's garage

The engine was collected from Pelletiere and again installed. But Vic never started it! Perhaps he thought it would be just as much fun exhibiting the racer at various locations and not risk driving it? Red became part of a special display in the Fort St. Joseph Museum in Niles during May of 1977. Red had no front wings and a large ribbed radiator hose ran from the Zoller's carburetor to the intake manifold.

One of Vic Hyde's dreams was to someday return Red to England and participate in a Silverstone meet with other Morgan trikes. Vic had been to Silverstone and drove Clarrie Coombes' Morgan on July 2, 1966 in event 9, the half hour trial for three wheelers and sidecars. He was presented a bronze plaque for completing 18 laps. Vic's dream to take Red to England, however, never materialized.

During his ownership of Red, Vic had several offers to sell it, most of them from England. One proposal was to exchange Red for a restored circa-1934 Morgan barrel back super sport. Vic was very fond of the barrel back body style, but feared the proposed owner would beat Red to death on the track, even though he was given written assurance to the contrary. He was very protective of Red and his fleet of three wheelers. That fear and the economic reality of transporting Red a distance of 3,000 miles determined that a British owner wouldn't acquire Red in 1974.

Vic Hyde and I met during my trip to Waterville, Maine in 1975 to purchase an unrestored 1931 Morgan JAP Super Aero from Jim Hartman. On the return trip to San Francisco, Vic spotted my Chevy barreling down Highway 80 towing the Morgan Aero on a snowmobile trailer. He was driving in the opposite direction, made an illegal U-turn, and gave chase. After pursuing for five miles he caught up and we had a nice roadside chat.

A visit to Vic's place in Niles allowed a view of Red and his great three wheeler collection. We shared a mutual admiration and fascination for three wheeled vehicles.

My first Morgan trike was a 1934 MX Family, purchased in 1970 in England. Over the years many three wheelers have inhabited the garage including 3 F-Models, 2 Anzani two speed Aeros, 2 JAP Aeros, an MX 4 Super Sports, a JAP Super Sports and 3 BSA three wheelers. Two of the BSAs had the twin motors; the other a four cylinder. It was during my ownership of two of the BSAs that the idea of Vic's possible interest in them developed. He had been searching for a BSA for his collection for several years, but couldn't seem to find one.

Since first seeing Red at Vic's place in 1975, the interest to have it join my stable of Morgan trikes had grown. Correspondence with Vic in early January of 1977 described the two BSAs in detail and suggested a swap for Red. Red wasn't being driven, although Vic certainly valued and appreciated its heritage. At that point not much of its racing history was known. In his reply, Vic mentioned that he always told the boys in England Red would one day return to its homeland because no American other than himself valued its history. Hopes soared when he didn't decline the offer for the two BSAs, simply stating that he was caught off guard. He would need some time to consider the offer to swap trikes.

Numerous letters were exchanged during the next several months and it seemed Vic really might be willing to exchange Red for the two BSAs! The more Vic referred to Red – describing the collection of photos, paraphernalia, parts and its history – the more intriguing it became and the greater the desire to own it. Finally, in early March 1977, he agreed to swap Red for the two BSAs.

During negotiations over Red, things had been heating up in England beginning in 1971 when Tom Wheatcroft had purchased Donington Park. Buildings were constructed to house a superb collection of single seater racing cars. The collection was opened to the public on March 16, 1973. It became one of the finest collections of its type in the world and certainly worth a visit. Housed in the same area was an excellent collection of British historic vehicles assembled by British Leyland. The entire museum complex was named The Donington Collection.

After an immense amount of red tape, numerous difficulties, and remodeling of the racing circuit, Donington Park reopened on Sunday, May 15, 1977 for a National Motorcycle Race. Eight races for motorcycles were listed in the program in the senior, lightweight, junior, super bike, and sidecar categories. The meet kicked off at 1:30 PM and was enjoyed by a

The restored Red in the snow at Vic Hyde's home

large crowd of spectators. Many old timers brought out their vintage bikes to enjoy the experience of just being part of the scene. The new Donington Park race circuit had a lap distance of 1.957 miles.

On Sunday, July 24, 1977, the VMCC along with the Pathfinders and Derby Motor Club, Ltd. sponsored the BP Vintage Motor Cycle Road Races. Morgan three wheelers were invited to race after such a long absence. With 7 events scheduled for that day, the fifth was an 8 lap race for three wheelers, and the seventh was a three wheeler invitational.

Event 5 heat number 1 listed five 4-cylinder Morgans and 8 motorcycle sidecars including Triumph, Velocette, BMW, Norton and BSA. A total of 19 Morgans participated in the practice on the smooth surface before they were flagged in. Only Dave Hodgson missed practice in his 1935 4-cylinder 1172 cc Ford Morgan due to a cracked sliding axle. He was later allowed to get in some practice before the race began.

The first heat of event 5 saw John Lidgate's Triumph take the lead for lap one. It was closely followed by P. Wilkinson's Triumph, and then 3 more sidecars before the first Morgan – Chris Weston's 1935 model. Dave Hodgson was right behind him in his 1935 Ford Morgan. John Rowland brought up the rear in his 1934 990 cc V-Twin Morgan. The leaders held their places through lap 2, but Hodgson passed Weston and was chasing Titch Allen on his 1939 520 Norton. Lap 3 saw Hodgson zip past Allen, but Pilbeam, in his 1948 Morgan F-Super, was coming up fast.

During lap 4, Hodgson moved into fourth place just behind Ron East on a 1938 600 Norton. Pilbeam was now running sixth and closing on Barbara and Michael Coombes on their 1951 650 Triumph. Back in the pack, Clifford Deardon was running ninth, with Roland tenth and Weston twelfth.

On lap 5, John Lidgate's Triumph was now beginning to lap the end runners. On lap 6 Hodgson was still running fourth with Pilbeam fifth. Clifford Deardon suffered a puncture of the rear wheel and was out of the race. Lap 7 saw Hodgson moving up to third place and Ron East fell back. Rosemary Wilkinson on her 1939 499 Velocette now brought up the rear. At the finish John Lidgate breezed home to an easy win on his 650 Triumph. Following him were Wilkinson on a 500 Velocette, then Hodgson with his Morgan. Allen, who lead for so long on his Norton, was fourth, and Pilbeam took fifth with his 1948 Morgan.

Heat number 2 of event 5 looked to be an exciting race for three wheelers with a turnout of 16 listed on the program. The announcer was so excited trying to describe the lineup he had difficulty finishing introductions before the race began. Following 1930s tradition, the Morgans were carrying passengers. The front row included Bill Tuer passengered by William Winstanley at the pole in his 1932 1100 cc trike, Gary Caroline in his 1928 1096 cc Morgan passengered by Nigel Allen, and Andy Stewart in his 1932 1100 cc Morgan. The front row was completed with Stuart Harper and Jonathan Garside in Stuart's popular 1922 Ware Replica 1000 cc Morgan.

Spectators watched as Tim Green pushed his Morgan but couldn't make the start. The remainder of the field was composed of driver - passengers: Geoffrey Belcher - Jill Belcher, Harold Pass - Peter Campbell, Martyn Bayliss - Malcolm Bull, Greg Bibby - Howard Chivrall, Nicholas Edwards - Alistair Parkes, Adrian and Patricia Murray-Leslie, Peter Enticknap - Charles Reynolds, and Dennis Rogers - George Gould.

Bill Wallbank with his ex-Tom Rhodes' Morgan was missing from the field. He was carrying out extensive repairs from an earlier accident. Bob Angell experienced the unfortunate loss of the rear main shaft on his 1930 1098 cc Morgan during practice and retired after enjoying 6 laps.

At the start, Caroline, Tuer, Stewart and Harper got off quickly with the pack trying to catch them. Caroline squeezed by Tuer at Holly Wood with Stewart and Harper close behind. Not more than a length of 3 Morgans separated them. Bringing up the group were Belcher, followed by Bibby, Enticknap and Pass.

Lap 2 was a close match for first between Caroline and Tuer with Harper now running third. Stewart had to withdraw with a seized engine. But wait, Harper went onto the grass at the old hairpin, struggled and regained control. Enticknap moved into fourth place followed in close order by Pass, Belcher, Bibby, Edwards and Bayliss.

During the third lap, Harper in the Ware Replica, retired with a holed piston. This still left Caroline in first with Tuer second and Pass had moved into third. The fourth lap was not too exciting, the thrills taking place in the fifth lap. Nick Edwards rolled his Morgan at Red Gate Lodge. While he suffered no injury, the Morgan was extensively damaged. Bill Tuer passed Gary Caroline to take the lead and held it to the end. The final results showed Tuer, Caroline, Pass, Enticknap, Belcher, Murray-Leslie and Bibby, finishing in that order.

Event 7 was an Invitational Eight Lap Race for three wheelers; 16 Morgans and 8 sidecars formed the field. The first 5 laps were led by John Lidgate on his 650 Triumph with Caroline and Tuer not far behind. At the end of the fifth lap, Caroline and Tuer surged ahead of Lidgate, building up a comfortable lead. Behind Lidgate were Wilkinson and Hodgson. On the final lap, Tuer just got past Caroline to take first. Third place was Lidgate's Triumph, Wilkinson's Velocette fourth and Hodgson's Morgan in fifth.

This event marked the first time that Morgans had been on the track at Donington since it closed 38 years earlier! Donington Park was back on the map and so was Morgan racing at that location.

Racing at Donington Park was still fun in modern times, but the atmosphere was not the same as in the days of the 1930s when Laird and Lones were on the track. Who knows, if Henry Laird were still with us, he might have been out there on the track watching today's young lions having their fun. Surely, he would have rejoiced in knowing that Red was destined to campaign again on the track.

Back in the States, the logistics of exchanging two BSAs for Red was a challenge due to Vic's busy schedule The decision was made to meet approximately halfway between Michigan and California. Denver was suggested, but after careful study of road maps, Cheyenne, Wyoming was chosen avoiding the traffic and hassle of going through Denver. Highway 80, the closest route between Niles and San Francisco, ran right through Cheyenne. The name of the town had a nice sound to it with Indian history and folklore, a part of the Old West.

With only one small trailer having three ramps – but two BSAs to transport – I was fortunate locating someone living 70 miles away who was going East with an empty trailer and could take the 1934 four-cylinder BSA trike. He had arrangements to pick up a Ford Model-T in Florida.

On the arranged day, all parties hit the highway hoping to meet in Cheyenne in four days' time. The weather was perfect and no one had any mishaps. On the morning of June 2, 1977, we pulled into The Locomotive Park, home of Big Boy, the World's Largest Steam Locomotive, built in 1941.

Red looked sparkling in bright red and exuded an appearance of moving while standing still – it was that front sloping cowl which gave it a sense of speed. Vic had driven his huge Vic Hyde Show enclosed trailer pulled by a large van. It would easily transport the two BSA trikes.

Vic's friend, Warren Kirkland, had driven 160 miles from his home to say hello and give us some support. It was an historic moment captured by cameras.

The author with Red and Vic with his two new B.S.A.s

Vic says good-bye to Red with a heartfelt kiss

Parting with Red was emotional for Vic and he planted a good-by kiss on the tail of the old racer. Parting with the BSAs was less emotional, but it was certainly exciting to be getting an historic racing Morgan! We waved a final good-by and headed in opposite directions down Highway 80.

While driving through the Bonneville Salt Flat area just West of Salt Lake City, an opportunity was seized to take photos of Red against that immense background of sparkling white sand. Impelled to stop by the Speedway Cafe, views were enjoyed of the photos on the walls showing those who attempted speed records on the salt. What would Henry Laird have thought about racing Red on the salt?

Making good time, there was an opportunity to visit Harrah's Auto Collection in Sparks, Nevada. A friend, Sandy Brighton, worked as a Bar Manager for Harrahs at the collection. We asked the Museum's Technical Advisor, Dean Batchelor, to come outside for a look at Red. He thought it was an interesting machine, but knew nothing about its history. The Harrah's Auto Collection was very impressive until the late 1970s; the auto museum was later acquired by Holiday Inn and underwent a major down sizing.

The remainder of the trip to San Francisco was without incident. Vic also had a trouble free trip home to Niles and made plans right away to take one of the BSAs on the road for his next musical assignment.

The '32 BSA and four of his other vehicles were scheduled for exhibit in Old Chicago, the shopping mall and amusement park a half hour drive from Chicago in Bolingbrook. By June 27, Vic was up in Thunder Bay, Ontario on another gig.

Several articles about "the BSAs for Red swap" appeared in the Morgan Three Wheeler Club's magazine, *The Bulletin*, and raised criticism, primarily aimed at Vic. The joke at the time pointed out that Vic had received the booby prize in his trade. Several of *The Bulletin* issues in 1977 registered an exchange between Vic and Barry Davidson regarding the subject. A lot of the bantering was tongue in cheek, but sparked an interest with several Morgan enthusiasts to acquire a BSA trike. Vic declared the motoring virtues and positive aspects of owning BSAs, giving them an excellent rating.

Time was spent looking over the newly acquired Morgan racer. At first there was hesitation to lay a spanner on Red. It was satisfying just admiring it. Reflecting on the sights it must have witnessed back in the 1930s – specifically while it was at Brooklands and Donington Park competing in speed events.

Close inspection of Red showed a foot throttle in place, front hydraulic brakes, and a generator bracket mounted on the gearbox. This bracket took up the space reserved for the other Hartford friction shock. The Hartford shock was in a box of parts so it could be installed without a problem. Red could be restored to its 1930s configuration and didn't require a generator.

Red in San Francisco, June 1977

Morgan owners Dick Tuttle and Jan Barton from San Jose stopped by to look over the new acquisition and view the photo album which John Lindop had painstakingly assembled. The lap racing charts penned by Barbara Laird were also of immense interest since they stated the tuning elements for the engine and listed the times and results for Red in all races entered while it was in Henry Laird's possession.

Before commencing with the restoration, Red required some parts, so a trip was planned to England. While there, more history was researched about the racer. Members of the Brookland's Society were contacted and an opportunity to join one of their weekend track clearings ended in hoeing weeds. Standing on the historic Brooklands site – imagining the sounds of racing machines barely muffled by their Brookland's cans – visualizing the colorful scenes which attracted so many people years before – this was the air, the ether of racing history: the drivers and owners who bravely warmed up their motors for a contest of speed; the spectators who came to watch and be watched; the ladies in their ankle-length flowing skirts which gradually rose to a shorter length exposing their knees; their large hats becoming small close-fitting styles with deep rounded crowns and narrow brims; the men dressed in derbies and scarves, carrying umbrellas. Such a lively past! It was sad now to see it all gone and view the condition of the site. Brooklands had been left to ruin by those who could have done something to preserve it.

During this trip to England in 1977, Titch Allen gave me a personal tour of the Stanford Hall Museum where I had a chance to see Yellow for the first time. He offered generous hospitality and we visited Harry Lomas and asked him a lot of questions about his involvement with Yellow and Red during the 1930s. His comments were recorded on audio cassette. Harry later visited the United States in 1980, and while in San Francisco provided more historical information about Red.

It was a special privilege to visit Richard Laird who recalled some of Red's history. In particular, he described the struggle he and Henry used to share when push starting the trike at Donington. The engine would occasionally fire on one cylinder which made the trike jump ahead about five yards. If Richard didn't react quickly and jump in he got left behind, or if he tripped or was caught off balance he could take a header. The 8:1 bottom gear ratio made coordination difficult when push starting. As a result of the trip to England, more history of the Red racer came to light and restoration of the trike could begin.

The goal was firmly established – to restore Red to its racing condition and put it back on the road. The JAP KTOR engine was delivered to Jan Barton to check over on June 28, 1977. Upon tearing it down, he found a residue of glass beading inside the cases and all of the internal engine components were loose. It was a good thing that Vic hadn't tried to start the engine as it could have come apart internally with disastrous results. The oilways would have soon plugged up with glass bead residue.

On July 2, 1977, Red's body was removed from the chassis and placed on a Morgan chassis restoration dolly designed by Joe Pearson of Chicago. This dolly rolled on casters which allowed the body (and later, the chassis) to be easily moved. Chassis components were painted red. The left front wheel had a broken spoke which was replaced by Bob Key, a wire wheel specialist. Motorcycle personality, Hap Jones, personally supplied new Avon SM MK II 350 by 19 tires. Dick Tuttle worked on reshaping the wind scallops and rebushing the Newton shocks fitted to the front suspension.

Hydraulic brakes were converted back to the cable type used by Henry Laird. The front brake pulley system was refurbished and installed with new fabricated parts. The foot throttle was removed and the throttle control cable returned to its location on the steering wheel.

Vic Hyde stayed in touch and continued to supply items for Red from his hoard of parts. The bronze heads, rocker arms, valves and other items arrived periodically by Greyhound packaging.

The Brooklands Gold Star wasn't received until September 12, 1979. When it arrived in a letter from Vic, I was surprised by its size. The Star is about the size of a dime and has 100 stamped on its front surrounded by blue porcelain. The letters "H. Laird" are engraved on the back. Four small eyelets are attached to corners of the star which attach to a larger pin or chain.

On November 19, 1982, another item arrived in the mail – Red's tow plate which had YY19 on one side, and RC 450 on the reverse. This was the British registration plate from the McEvoy Special which doubled as the racer's towing sign.

While more information was coming to light about Red's past, the chassis was painted and assembled. It looked great in a bright red enamel. Word had spread throughout the Morgan community about progress on the racer's restoration and an invitation was received to display it at ISIS on Pier 33 in San Francisco on August 24, 1978 for their Grand Opening. At that time, Bill Fink's ISIS dealership was the only firm in the U.S. selling new Morgans.

A gathering of Morgan owners viewed the chassis that day and asked when the trike would be on the road; and, moreover, back on the track to reclaim its

Red alongside the nice 1952 Morgan +4 racer owned by Jim Belardi

racing heritage. Their enthusiasm was instrumental in the continuation with the restoration.

The engine work continued in Jan Barton's garage. The crank pin assemblies were overhauled and the internal flywheels checked and trued. Some camshaft and roller parts were obtained from England and delivered to Jan on October 12, 1979.

On May 26, 1981, the engine was ready for installation on the chassis. It had taken from June 1977 until March 1982 to complete the restoration. Jan came to offer advice and left some notes. Adjustments were made to the carburetor, brakes and gear shift gate controls. The exhaust system was revamped and gave Red a nice look.

April 9, 1982 – the engine was fired up and Red driven under its own power. Less than 10 miles had been put on the racer during the past 25 years. Several were logged that day!

The racer was entered in several shows during 1982. These included: San Francisco's One Market Plaza Auto Show March 22-27; Morgans on The Lawn V in Fullerton, CA on April 18; the Hillsborough Concours on May 16; Second Annual Mare Island Auto Show in the antique motorcycle class for a 2nd place award on May 22; the Silverado Concours on June 6 for a 3rd place; the Lafayette Concours for a 2nd place, July 11; and the Hayward Rotary Concours for a 1st place on July 25. A number of people in the Bay Area were getting to view Red, the retired racer. Vic Hyde was proud of the fact that Red was being displayed.

Two days after the Hayward show, the external flywheel shifted, causing some damage to the big end key way on the mainshaft. More lessons were learned about installing the external flywheel. With the damage repaired, the flywheel was carefully lapped on to the big end shaft and secured with Locktite. A long pipe over the end of a wrench provided enough torque to securely tighten the big end nut. It didn't slip again!

Red was driven on occasion and again exhibited in 1983: May 22, at the Hillsborough Concours, a 3rd place award; June 5, Silverado Concours, no award; Palo Alto Concours on June 19, a 3rd place; Lafayette Concours July 10, a first place; July 23 a filming stint in Bodega Bay with a rock group for a music video; September 11, the Walnut Creek Concours for 3rd place; and October 2, the First Winner's Circle display at Strybing Arboretum in Golden Gate Park.

An artist from *Road and Track* thought Red was impressive and did a water color sketch which ended up on the content's page of the Vol. 34, No. 10 issue of June 1983.

In 1984 the Morgan Factory celebrated their 75th Anniversary of vehicle manufacture. At Laguna Seca in Monterey on May 18-20, the Morgan Clubs of Northern and Southern California staged a special event to commemorate the occasion. Red was carefully prepared and road tested for this event. The magneto was overhauled with a new coil to provide a reliable, strong spark. The 19 tooth gearbox sprocket was changed to one with 17 teeth. A new Carlisle 400 X 19 tire was fitted on the rear wheel. Engine valves were adjusted. The main jet was changed from 240 to 260 in the Amal monobloc. Red's body received paint touch up. A friend and Morgan owner, Charles Artel, donated a racing seat belt.

Everything appeared ready and Red arrived at the Laguna Seca track on May 18. During practice on May 19 after 13 laps the engine developed a rattling noise. The timing chest appeared to be the source – something had come loose. This incident ended racing for the weekend, although it was still a special event for Red to be at the track after such a long absence. Several days later the engine was pulled off the frame for examination. The number two cam had come loose. A shaft connecting it to the oil pump drive had threads cut in the wrong direction. The pounding of the cam cracked the fragile front engine case in several places. Too many fractures existed for a satisfactory repair and a set of new cases were required. A search began which lasted for a number of months. Finally a replacement set of cases was obtained from Bob Thredder in England. A machinist friend, George Tollworthy, corrected the front drive threads on the number two camshaft. The engine was then reassembled and installed. It took until January of 1987 to complete the work. Red had been off the road this time for two years and seven months.

In 1987, Red was taken to the Bi-Annual Friendship Day meet on May 17; the Silverado Concours on June 7; on June 28, the River City Concours secured a 1st place award for retired racing cars. Lastly, Red was entered in the Lafayette Concours on July 12 and then went into storage until April 1988. It wouldn't be raced until more was learned about the engine and how to make it dependable. Meanwhile, perhaps it was best to be satisfied with displaying it as Vic Hyde had done.

During late April of 1988 Red's interior woodwork was repainted in gray and the racing seat belt was removed. Attention to smaller items was carried out the following month. It was now running well and entered in the Greater Valley Concours in Fresno on May 15. No awards were won at this show but spectators thought it an interesting exhibit.

Plans were made to take it to the annual Mog West event at Cambria in July. That event was the premier West Coast gathering of Morgans each year sponsored by the Northern and Southern California Morgan Clubs. Many of the Morgan owners and enthusiasts from both clubs had not previously seen Red and it created quite an interest during the concours. At the event banquet it was awarded Best of Show. Following this event, Red again went into storage so other projects could move forward.

On October 17, 1989 there was *a whole lot of shaking going on* when the San Andreas Fault moved suddenly and violently beneath Central California. The rental garages where Red was stored were in San Francisco's Marina District one mile from the site where buildings collapsed and fires raged. In Red's garage a cinder block dislodged and made a large crease in the left side exhaust pipe. Fortunately that was the only damage to Red and his stablemates – my apartment was another matter. I had to vacate it for two months and move the trikes to a friend's garage. It was time to move out of the Marina and take the cars to a safer location. At the time two other Morgan trikes, a 1929 Darmont Family model and a prize winning 1930 JAP Aero, which was affectionately called Strawberry, were also in rented Marina garages.

Unexpectedly, a phone call was received from Bob Thredder in England asking if Red might be for sale. During my last visit to England we had discussed this possibility and I told him it wasn't for sale. How one's fortunes and circumstances can change! The timing was right for his call and we would now deal if he also took the other two trikes. Bob promised to give an answer in a couple of days. He was in the process of selling another car and thought he could raise the cash. When he phoned back and said he could, an emotional wave sweep over me. Not really wanting to part with the Red, the prize of my Morgan collection, how could I now withdraw the offer? We closed the deal and shipping was arranged.

Red and the other two Morgan trikes left San Francisco on January 26, 1990. Included in the sale to Bob were photo albums, lap racing charts penned by Barbara Laird, assorted literature items, the Brooklands Gold Star, and the damaged bronze engine cases and Baronia bronze heads.

Sent by sea in one large shipping container, the three Morgans arrived safely at their British destination. Red had returned to English soil after a 29 year leave! While it was in the United States, there were dreams of returning it to England for a reunion with the Lones' and Rhodes' trikes which had been Red's teammates for the Brooklands LCC Relay Races. Red should make an appearance at one of the Brooklands Reunions. It should also return to Donington Park to

The Clive Lones Morgan when owned by Alan Goldsmith

visit its old haunts. Earlier, several airlines had been approached for sponsorship. Tom Wheatcroft, who owned Donington Park, was contacted but the plan found no support. Now that Red was back in England, it would be Bob Thredder's responsibility to see what he could accomplish. His personality seemed to indicate he would drive and display it and at least take it to Brooklands.

One of Bob's ambitions was to restore Red's bronze JAP engine. He had a sample of the metal removed from the bronze cases which was examined by a metallurgist and analyzed by computer. From that data, welding rods were created with the same material composition used in the cases. These rods were used to weld the cases damaged by Hugh Dyer 30 years earlier when he blew up the engine. Alec Card of JAP Industries assembled the rods, bearings and flywheels of the bronze JTOR engine. Another of Bob's friends worked on the top end, i.e. the barrels and pistons.

The Zoller supercharger was inspected and repaired. The front wheels were given replacement spokes. New flame red paint was applied to the body. The cracked rear view mirror, in place when Red was shipped, was not replaced.

While the bronze engine was being rebuilt, Bob mounted the Zoller behind the old KTOR engine as a nonfunctional interest item and drove Red in this manner. To do this, he had to reverse the direction of the Amal carburetor, facing it forward.

Bob continued to use Red as his busy work schedule allowed. He took Red to a Brooklands Reunion where it received a lot of attention from other Morgan owners. The August 1990 issue of *The Automobile*, Vol. 8, No. 6, did a nice story with color photos on Red's return to England. One of the magazine photos showed Red on the track surface at Brooklands.

Between 1990-95, race meets at Laguna Seca and Sears Point provided the camaraderie of Morgan drivers and the competition of Morgan three wheelers. Seeing the pre-war group of cars racing at Laguna Seca in the famed Monterey Historics was always a special joy. There were usually 3 to 6 Morgan trikes attending this meet. Interest resulted in producing a video about Morgan three wheeler racing history. The more races attended, the stronger became my determination to acquire another Morgan and go racing. What machine would be suitable? Not just any Morgan would satisfy my desires. To be competitive, I wanted something special. Red would have filled that requirement but it was gone.

Recalling an old Morgan seen 15 years earlier in Sacramento, the owner's name was located in a roster of Morgan owners. John Gormley answered his phone and said he still owned an Aero model but it wasn't for sale. He intended to restore it some day. How often have those words been spoken? At any rate, we kept in touch during the next several months and he was offered a price for the trike. John stated that another person had already approached him and had first refusal. The purchase price had already been determined. The other person was scheduled to inspect the Aero in several days. When the other person saw the Morgan they were shocked at how much work it needed and tried knocking down the price. John was so incensed that he phoned and asked if I were still interested at his price. Several days later we made a trip to Sacramento and returned with a 1932 JAP Aero.

As far as was known, no one in the U.S. was racing an Aero model. It would be unusual to say the least – its high tail body exposing much of the rear wheel. This old Aero was in sad condition, requiring a lot of attention. The direction of the work was clear. It would require a complete stripping of the chassis down to the last nut and bolt. Work commenced.

The chassis was sanded to bare metal, inspected for cracks, then primed and painted. This was a time consuming and tedious process. A period of two years was required before the completed trike was road worthy and ready to show. During the restoration process Donna Dell'Ario ably assisted with the chassis restoration and helped create the color scheme. She fabricated a new dashboard using the existing pattern and did all the layout and sewing for the top, tonneau and engine covers.

The engine was overhauled by Ray Olsen in Eureka. Donna helped produce a video during the fabrication and restoration of the sheet metal with work performed by Ron Covell. All of the final assembly was done at home in the garage and the finished product showed a lot of attention to detail. The newly restored trike was christened *Old Rose* because of its color scheme in maroon and green.

The 1932 Morgan Aero was finished in December 1995. It was displayed at the *Motor Cycle* magazine's Readers' Collection exhibit in San Mateo during January of 1996. The restoration was completed only a week prior to that show. Since it was the only Morgan entered – labeled a cycle car – it drew a lot of attention and took home a first place award in the Specials Class.

Old Rose was taken to Mog West in July of 1996. At the concours, it was awarded a first place. It was campaigned in the speed event at the Hearst Castle Airstrip and took another first in class. While this three wheeler was nice and proving to be popular with Morgan enthusiasts, it was not destined to be the next entry for the race track. The Aero's narrow width and high ground clearance would have perhaps made it competitive with Yellow on a hill climb, but it wasn't set up properly for race track competition. For racing, the chassis would require widening and lowering.

Prior to this plans had been made to attend the 1995 celebration of the 50th Anniversary of the founding of The Morgan Three Wheeler Club in Great Malvern, England. Perhaps a presentable racing Morgan would become available during that trip? Realizing that Red was the only Morgan to fulfill my plans to go racing – I had to accept the fact that it wasn't for sale. Bob Thredder, however, planned to participate with it in the Morgan anniversary weekend celebrations. With the finished bronze engine in place, it would present a formidable sight. Was it finally time for Red's reunion with the trikes of Tommy Rhodes and Clive Lones who raced with it in the 1930s?

As the date drew near Bob was having difficulty getting Red running. When the bronze engine was installed, the prop shaft length wasn't properly measured. It was too long. The engine was bolted onto the chassis and the prop shaft's extra length put excessive stress on the rear plug of the gearbox breaking the housing. A replacement gearbox was located but time ran out before it could be delivered and installed. Red would not make an appearance at the 50th Anniversary event. The historic racing trikes of Lones' and Rhodes' would have to appear without Laird's Red.

The 50th MTWC Anniversary Celebrations were outstanding. Although typical rainy English weather prevailed during part of the weekend, the event's overall success was fantastic. Can you picture an event with 200 Morgan three wheelers on display in a field behind the Morgan Factory? A superb banquet, luncheons, a speed event, concours and tours provided a constant opportunity for enthusiasts and spectators to revel in the glory of a slice of Morgan history. Additional pleasures came by having a chat with Titch Allen and being able to see Laird's Yellow on display. Yellow looked spartan and was displayed with a sign stating some of its history. Titch and his son look after this historic Morgan trials machine.

On May 28, there was an event at Cadwell Park which featured Morgans racing against motorcycle sidecars. Three Morgan trikes driven by Bill Tuer, Bob Angell, and Charles Reynolds demonstrated how three wheelers and sidecars did it back in the 1930's. The sidecars with their passengers (monkeys) put on

The 1932 JAP Aero affectionately named Old Rose

The dashboard shows additional gauges fitted during Red's stay in England 1990-1995

A non-working model of Red's bronze JAP JTOR engine made by a British artist. It measures 4" high and 3 3/4" wide

a great show! What a charge! Until you see the sidecar monkeys shifting their weight from side to side on the motorcycle platforms through every turn and down the straights you haven't seen action!

Several days later another race meet was held at Silverstone. The Morgan trikes of Gary Caroline and Bob Towell challenged each other and other pre-war cars around the circuit.

Toward the end of the trip, my itinerary included a visit with Bob Thredder to inspect his progress in solving Red's gearbox problem. An appointment was made to visit him in the South London dock area at his auto restoration facility. Bentley cars occupied many of his repair and restoration bays. Red sat over on one side of the garage looking a bit neglected with its engine off to one side. Bob had located a replacement gearbox but it hadn't been delivered. The broken one he had removed didn't look very healthy. Bob appeared so busy during this time that he didn't know when he would get Red running again. During his ownership of Red, he had installed additional vintage gauges on the facia panel. These included a black 2.25 inch Smiths time clock, a 5 inch brass speedometer and a 3 inch tachometer. An additional item was a rectangular brass plaque which read Brooklands Motors. All of the instruments looked nice and added to the vintage racing look.

The subject of buying Red back was approached and Bob wasn't totally opposed to the idea. Earlier, a phone call from Stan Thorpe had alerted me that Atlantic Motorcycles was advertising Red for the sum of 40,000 Pounds. Bob stated that he was not responsible for the ad. He said it had been placed by a speculator who was after some quick bucks and was done without his knowledge, although Bob didn't exactly disapprove when he saw the advertisement.

At this time, Bob was considering moving his wife and family into a larger home and relocating his car restoration business. Some quick cash could be very helpful. We bartered back and forth, considered what he had spent on Red's engine restoration, and discussed other factors.

Since 1993 – several years after Red was sold to Bob – my plan was to stay in touch with him regarding how he was using Red, its running condition, and the facts about the restoration of the bronze engine. A request was made for first refusal if he should decide to part with the racer. He realized that my desire to own Red wasn't for speculative purposes but only to participate with it in vintage racing. With this knowledge, Bob agreed to sell Red back to me, although with some reservation.

The next day we finalized the deal. I gathered up the photo books and various literature, the Brooklands Gold Star, and purchased a scale model of the bronze JTOR engine that a friend of Bob's had built. These items flew to San Francisco with me the following day.

During negotiations with Bob Thredder to repurchase Red, another of its former owners, Vic Hyde, was diagnosed with a brain tumor. He had been in ill health for some time, therefore unable to attend the Morgan Three Wheeler Club's Golden Anniversary in England. He would surely approve of my plans to return Red to vintage racing.

The New Millennium, 1995-Present

By prior arrangement, Bob Thredder built a wooden shipping crate for Red for air freight to San Francisco. We were not going to chance any damage or pilferage shipping it by sea. Red arrived back in the U.S. on July 26, 1995. Red would now get to share a garage with Old Rose in the home that its sale in 1990 helped finance.

The trike was securely packed for its air freight journey to San Francisco from England

It was sad news to hear in September that Vic Hyde had passed away in a nursing home. He was 83. He would have been proud knowing Red would be raced again with the engine Henry Laird used in the 1930s. Vic's spirit might be riding in the passenger seat during Red's first race.

Red's refurbishing began in late June by acquiring a gearbox case supplied by Paul Lukes, an ex-Morgan trike owner. Skip Kelsey, an MG specialist, provided a new clutch cover and disk. The clutch and flywheel went to Ray Olsen for balancing.

Red uses a "D" gearbox. Note the Hartford shocks mounted over the leaf springs

Red's old gearbox had been rigged together prior to shipment from England so the trike could be rolled into the shipping crate. The gears from the old box were removed for inspection and all appeared to be in good condition. New bearings and seals went into the replacement case. The gears were replaced in the case and it was installed on the chassis.

There was additional work. The right front wheel needed a new tapered roller bearing. The old Brooklands Cans were never very good and now showed metal fatigue. It was decided that Red needed cans closer to the original 1930s look. Dick Tuttle came to the rescue and fabricated a new pair of cans using a volumetric formula for the motor's cc capacity. The new Brooklands Cans were a definite improvement, keeping the correct style and producing a sound suitable for Red's vintage.

With the gearbox installed, the engine was bolted on to the chassis to determine the correct length for the prop shaft. The length of the shaft had to be exact so the drive sprocket on the motor's bell housing could line up with the one on the Zoller supercharger. Since the position of the Zoller on the chassis was fixed, the only adjustment for sprocket alignment was by moving the engine's position. The engine could be adjusted in or out on the chassis with shims. The trial and error of fitting the engine on the chassis numerous times finally resulted in the correct alignment of the Zoller and flywheel sprockets. The prop shaft was adjusted to the correct length by cutting it to length and silver soldering its splined end in place. The splined end fits through the clutch into the pilot bearing and flywheel.

The plan was to run the supercharger, more for effect than anything else. At the same time there were reser-

Rolling chassis with JAP JTOR bronze engine in place

The Zoller is mounted behind the engine. Note the chain drive and the Amal TT carburetor with dual float chambers

Road test March 2, 1996. Dick Tuttle adjusts the oil feed to the Zoller compressor

vations fearing the unreliability of old items like the Zoller. Performance is unpredictable when a drive chain is employed and extra oil lines have to be plumbed for the supercharger bearings. The decision was made to run with the supercharger and see what happened, but it was definitely a gamble.

Red was ready to be tested on February 26, 1996. The engine started for the first time with the Zoller connected. The garage filled with Red's lusty roar and clouds of white smoke. How convenient that the kill switch still worked! After patching leaks in the exhaust system, and starting without fogging the atmosphere, Red was rolled into the street and showed there was definitely life left in the old racer! Upon returning to the garage, the brakes were adjusted and a road test was scheduled.

March 2 was the date for the actual road test on a favorite country test road down the peninsula. Dick Tuttle came along to passenger in Red. Everything began well and went smoothly for the first few miles. Then the exhaust valve stuck open on the number two head. The piston in that cylinder also seized. A quick shut down kept the engine from serious damage. We coasted to the roadside and discussed whether the clearances in the guides were correct. The piston clearances were also suspect. Another growing concern was that the bronze heads were not properly fitted. Red was loaded up and returned home.

The bronze heads were removed and sent to Ray Olsen. His mechanic made new seats and fitted new valves in both heads. The seized piston was sent to Venolia Pistons for replacement. More clearance was definitely required. A larger jet was installed in the carburetor for better cooling and supercharger performance.

While the heads were being reconditioned and new pistons were being forged, a dozen other little items required attention. The rotary oil valve was checked and reset. The brake cables were shortened and adjusted. Donna made a pattern and sewed a tonneau cover. This cover would provide good protection when trailering Red to events.

Application was made to the Historic Motor Sports Association (HMSA) for participation in two races: the Mollie Stone's Markets Wine Country Classic at Sears Point Raceway on June 7-9, 1996 and the Chrysler Corporation's 23rd Annual Monterey Historic Automobile Races at Laguna Seca on August 16-18, 1996. There was a little concern that even if we were accepted Red wouldn't be ready.

On April 11, the heads arrived from Ray. The new valve assemblies looked good and hopefully would be dependable for a long time. A few days later oil lines were installed from the Pilgrim oil pump to the rocker boxes for guide lubrication. This setup was copied from the configuration used on the Rhodes' trike.

May 15 arrived and the engine was ready to fire. The starter button was depressed and the engine roared to life. It sounded great. A check was made for any exhaust or oil leaks and these given attention before any actual road testing.

By May 25 all systems were looking good and the trike was taken out for a road test south of San Francisco. Red ran well for several miles and was fun to drive with the Zoller spinning away furiously – the chains and sprockets madly whirring. Was this the sound Henry Laird experienced when he drove Red? The beautiful thump, burble, thump, burble, thump, thump from the big JAP was like music! Aware that the engine needed breaking in, the temptation was resisted to open up the engine and see what Red could actually do. The 2 inch brass air pressure gauge which Dick Tuttle supplied was indicating a reading from the Zoller. Zipping down the roadway, Red was close to 50 mph when a sharp rattle echoed from the Zoller. The magneto kill toggle was quickly flipped to off and the clutch was depressed. The engine locked up solid as the trike coasted to a stop! Close inspection revealed that the supercharger case had cracked in several places and chunks of it were lying on the chassis. Hopefully, the engine had shut off before any damage had occurred to the heads or pistons. What a charge driving Red with the Zoller working and what a disappointment that it broke.

Back home, the engine was pulled off and the intake tubes removed. Chunks of aluminum had been sucked along the induction tube from the supercharger into the heads. One chunk, about the size of a quarter, lay in the intake tube right before the intake valve. When the heads were removed, there was no apparent damage to either the valves or seats. The engine had been shut off in time to prevent a disaster! Of course, the crankcase was drained as a precaution and the heads thoroughly cleaned along with all valve passages. Poor Red! Another delay in becoming race worthy.

Perhaps the Zoller could be rebuilt at a later date? The engine would now be fitted with carburetors. Two of them. Dennis Magri, owner of a motorcycle

The Baronia bronze cylinder head showing the exhaust valve, left, and the intake next to the 90° manifold

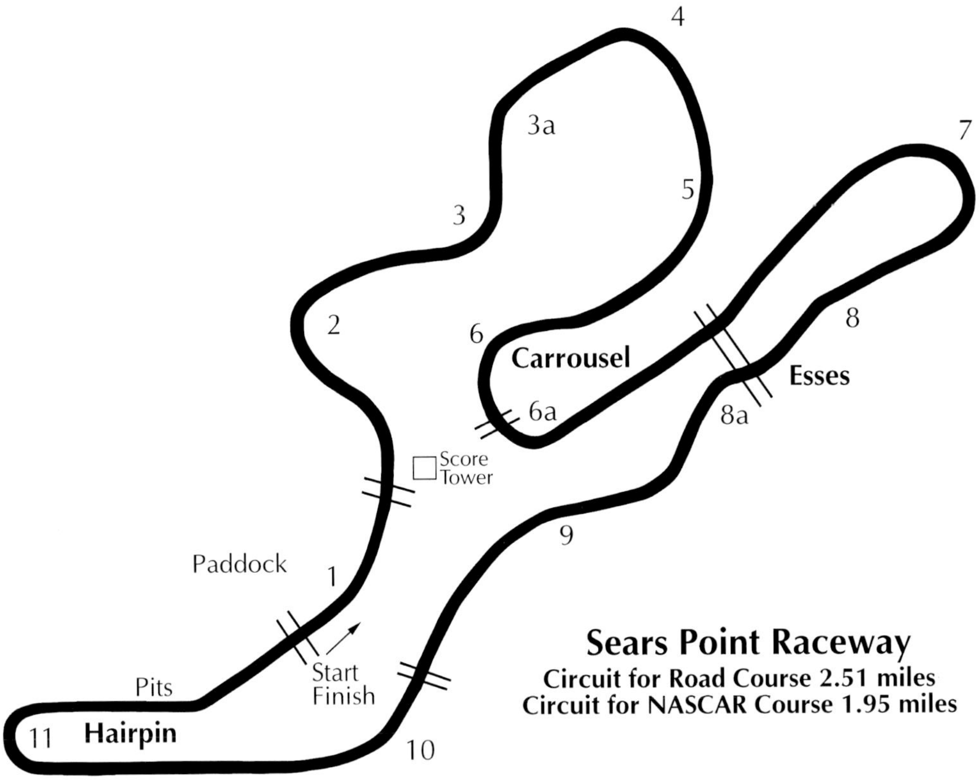

repair facility, supplied a pair of 30 mm Amal concentrics. Using adapters obtained through a Triumph motorcycle dealership, the dual carburetors were fitted with rubber hoses and screw clamps to the intake elbows. It took a little time to set up the throttle cables and adjust them to the hand control. The carbs opposed each other because of tight clearances between the cylinders. One faced to the front and the other to the rear of the engine. The engine should breath clean so air filters were installed on the carburetors. Air cleaners are always recommended. If anyone has researched the subject they have some idea of the volume of impurities that can be sucked into the engine through the carburetors.

Work was progressing. Donna applied the racing numbers 151 on either side of the rear body panels. These were the identical numbers displayed by Henry Laird when he raced Red at Donington Park in 1937 and are clearly shown in several of the period race photos. Donna also designed Red Morgan Racing logo patches for the new red jump suits that would become our pit uniforms. She became the official Pit Crew Chief.

The Zoller supercharger following the May 1996 testing incident

On June 4, 1996 Red was road tested only a few days before the HMSA 10th Annual Mollie Stone's Wine Country Classic at Sears Point. The track, situated among rolling hills, has some dramatic changes in elevation which affords a challenge to drivers and a pleasant view for spectators who can catch the aroma of the fuel and tires from the track, but at certain times of the year, breathe in the aroma of grapes from the nearby vineyards. Overall, a most pleasant experience.

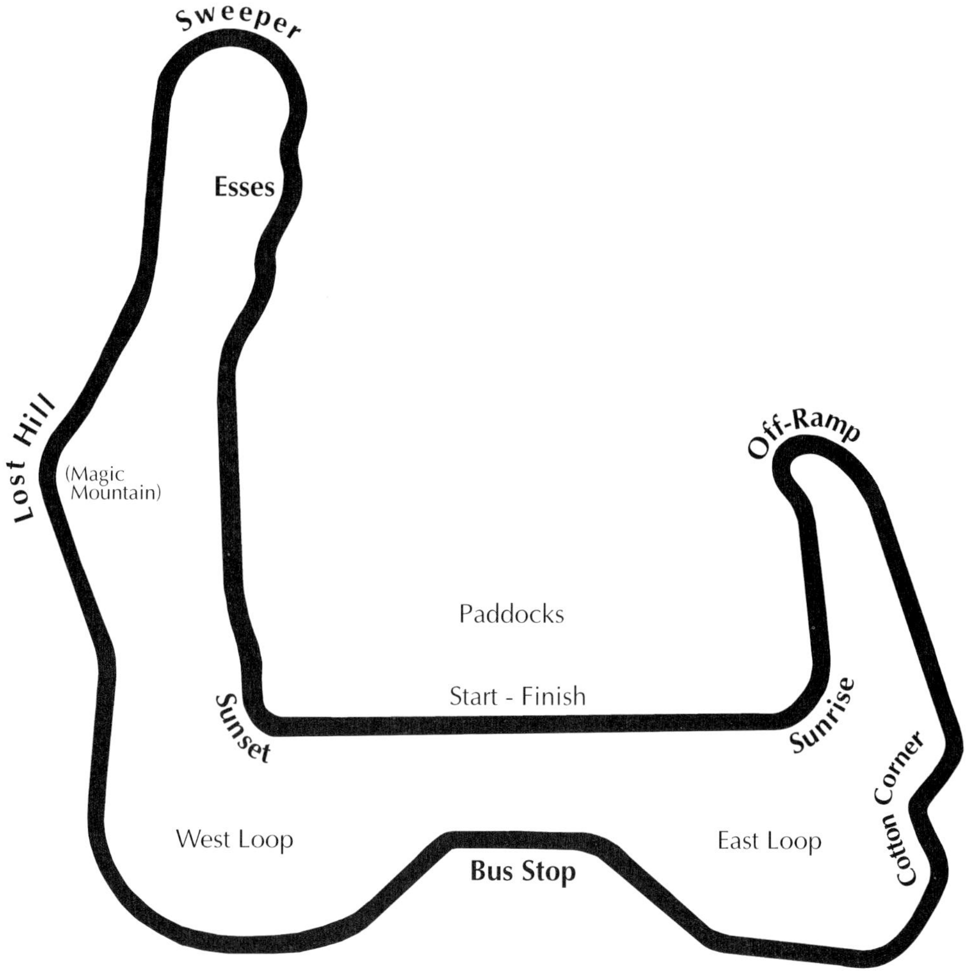

Buttonwillow Raceway Park
2.92 miles with 21 turns

Other Morgan trikes entered in Red's group were those driven by Alan Moss, Gary Byrd and Spence Young. Group One was for 1914-1954 Sports and Racing Cars, so Morgans were in the same class with cars of much larger size and displacement. The group contained a total of 28 entries including a 1951 Hudson Hornet, 1959 Mercedes-Benz 300 SL, 1959 Berkeley B95, and a 1952 Jaguar XK-120.

A notebook was purchased so Red's pertinent racing facts could be recorded such as engine specifications, work performed, lap times, and race results. Our modern day method followed that used by Barbara Laird when she recorded Red's 1930s racing campaigns. Donna was continuing the tradition began by Barbara sixty years earlier.

Red's JTOR engine was running bronze cases and heads with the spark provided by a Lucas magneto firing NGK B7ES plugs. The fuel tank was filled with Shell 89 fuel and the oil tank with Penrite HPR 40. The results of previous testing determined the following set up for Red's first excursion back on the race track. The twin Amals were fitted with mains of 180 in number one and 220 for the number two cylinder with a 106 needle in the middle notch in each instance. The gearbox was fitted with a 19 tooth drive sprocket. Avon 350 x 19 SM MK II tires were on the front, a Carlisle 400 x 19 on the rear.

The weather was warm and balmy but quite pleasant. The pit crew consisted of Donna Dell'Ario and Dick Tuttle. Other friends stopped by throughout the weekend to offer good luck.

During practice on Saturday, Red ran in a 3 min. 17 through 23 sec. range. Qualifying was nearly the same, but the engine felt like it was tightening up during each uphill climb at turns 3 and 3A. On one lap, it nearly seized, but ran better as soon as we passed the crest of the hill. The constant threat of engine seizure kept the trike from being very competitive. Red averaged 3 min. 33.38 sec. for its five qualifying laps. An even better time was recorded for the race the following day with a 3 min. 16.57 sec. average.

Sears Point, June 8, 1996: Larry in Red followed by Al Moss – 1934 Morgan MX4 SS, Graham Wallis – 1929 Lagonda. *Photo Bob Dunsmore*

Larry provides Red's first American class win at Buttonwillow, June 15, 1996

One Morgan in Red's group, the 1934 MX4 SS Trepenpol Special driven by Spence Young broke a timing pinion and he was out of the final race. This was the first time in 14 years of racing that Spence wasn't able to make the final event on race day! The other Morgans finished with no mishaps and overall everyone considered the weekend very successful.

We celebrated this event with Red, documenting its return to racing. The first time it had been on the track since 1984, an absence of 12 long years – and the first time it had completed a race since 1951!

Red was entered in the inaugural British Extravaganza, conducted by the Vintage Auto Racing Association (VARA) on June 14-16, 1996. The site was the new Buttonwillow Raceway Park located between Buttonwillow and Lost Hills, California. This was a new track built in an area of sagebrush and arid terrain. In April and May, before the temperatures begin soaring, the experience of racing there can be very comfortable. The track has some changing elevations with an interesting 3 mile layout consisting of 22 turns driven in either a clockwise or counterclockwise direction.

The weather at the track was hot, hovering around 95 degrees. Donna recorded lap times and looked after the base camp within the paddock area. Since I had not previously participated in a VARA event, Red was placed in the race group for novice drivers. The chassis and engine were set up as in the previous meet. The novice race on Saturday ran four laps. There were no other Morgans to run against, just MGs, Triumphs, Sprites and Austins.

Race Central recorded average lap times of 3 min. 29.37 seconds. The following day Red ran three laps in practice averaging 3 min. 43.58 seconds. Later that day in the Flag Race Red managed a time of 3 min. 24.89 seconds. That time was good enough to win the H-Mod class and Red was presented its first checkered flag! The JAP engine didn't exhibit any tendency toward seizing as it had in the earlier event at Sears Point.

Following the Buttonwillow meet, Red was thoroughly cleaned and given more road testing, tuning, and preparation. The racer was now running well enough that no major work had to be performed and it was ready for the Monterey Historics at Laguna Seca in August.

Laguna Seca Raceway is owned by the County of Monterey and is really a county park. It is operated by the Sports Car Racing Association of the Monterey Peninsula (SCRAMP), a non-profit organization. It is built on a 550 acre parcel comprising track, roadways and rolling hills. The layout has the largest elevation change in the shortest distance of any race course in the world. The corkscrew or turns 8 and 8A, have a drop off equivalent to a 5 story building. On November 9, 1957 the track conducted its first sports car race. The first Indy Car race was held on October 23, 1983. In 1988 the track was expanded from a 9-turn, 1.9 mile layout to one of 11 turns and 2.214 miles to

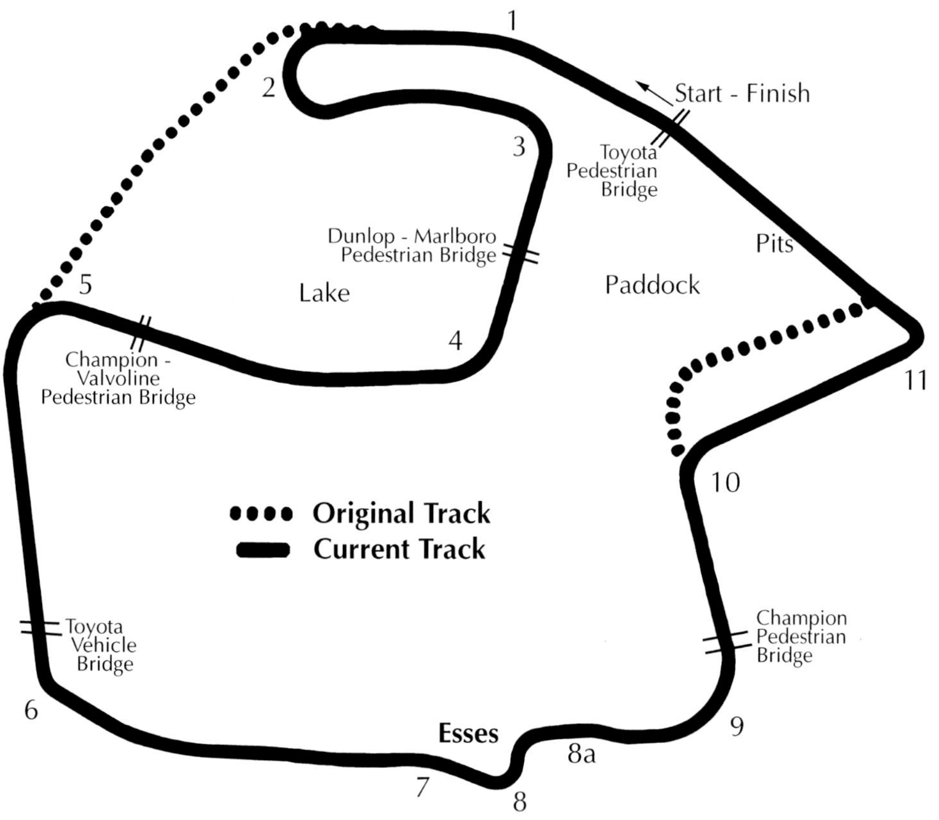

Laguna Seca Raceway
Original Track: 9 turns, 1.9 miles
1988: 11 turns, 2.214 miles • 1995: 11 turns, 2.238 miles

conform to international racing requirements. During 1995, the course was repaved and lengthened to 2.238 miles with the area between turns 10 and 11 expanded.

On August 15 Red was trailered up that steep grade from highway 68 to the track entrance. Pausing to absorb the ambiance – there lay ahead one of the most beautiful sights in the racing world. Within the center of the track a blue lake sparkled – nestled among rolling hills. The outlying hills neatly framed a setting fit for the world's greatest to drive upon. A racing paradise. A place where the scent of pine trees vied with Castrol R and racing fuel to create a heady mix. The place was magic and we were there to experience it all and to test both machine and driver. Red had made it – all the way from Brooklands to Laguna Seca!

Morgan Camp Three was set up and Red was unloaded. It was soon time to start the big JAP and head to the tech area. Red breezed through tech and we then had time to visit with the other entrants.

After attending the driver's school on Thursday, Red got some track time. Red's race group 2A included 1914-1940 Sports Racing Cars. On Friday, Spence Young in his Morgan led Red around the circuit during a 25 minute practice session, generously showing me the line. This is typical of the camaraderie shared between drivers.

Red was on the track for a total of 20 min. 12 sec. averaging 2 min. 49.66 sec. for 7 laps. The fastest lap was the last at 2 min. 47.11 seconds. Not as fast as your proverbial speeding bullet, yet not as slow as a third of the group. The newly surfaced track was a pleasure to drive and turns 8 and 8A provided the same thrill with that elevator drop as it did back in 1984.

Donna Dell'Ario headed our pit crew comprised of her brother, Dennis Olson and his wife Sharon, visiting from Colorado Springs. Weather throughout the weekend was comfortably warm with morning fog and afternoon breezes.

Early Saturday morning the front tires were checked for 30 psi with 35 in the rear and were ready to race. The 20 minute warm up session began at 9:20. This was actually the qualifying exercise for the race later in the day. For some reason Red was posting times

Sliding through the famous "corkscrew" at Laguna Seca leading a 1919 Miller TNT and 1947 Morgan F-Super at the Monterey Historics August 16 - 18, 1996. *Photo Bob Dunsmore*

The Red Morgan racing team at Laguna Seca. Left to right: Sharon Olson, Dennis Olson Donna Dell'Ario and Larry Ayers. To the left of Red is the 1934 Morgan JAP SS of Dale Barry

slower than the previous day. Four laps were timed from 2:49.61 to 3:00.37. Red would have energy to spare for the main event.

The 10 lap race was scheduled for 1:30 following lunch. The slower vehicles and the Morgans might achieve 7 or 8 laps. The group included some fast company including several BMW 328s – BMW was the featured marque for the weekend. This group also included a 1933 Alfa Romeo, 1930 Austin 7, 1934 Beavis Riley Special, 1914 Mercer, 1919 Miller TNT, several Ford Model Ts and 5 Morgan trikes, a field of 30 starters. Morgan three wheelers were driven by Allen Naille ('47 F-Super, 100E), Spence Young

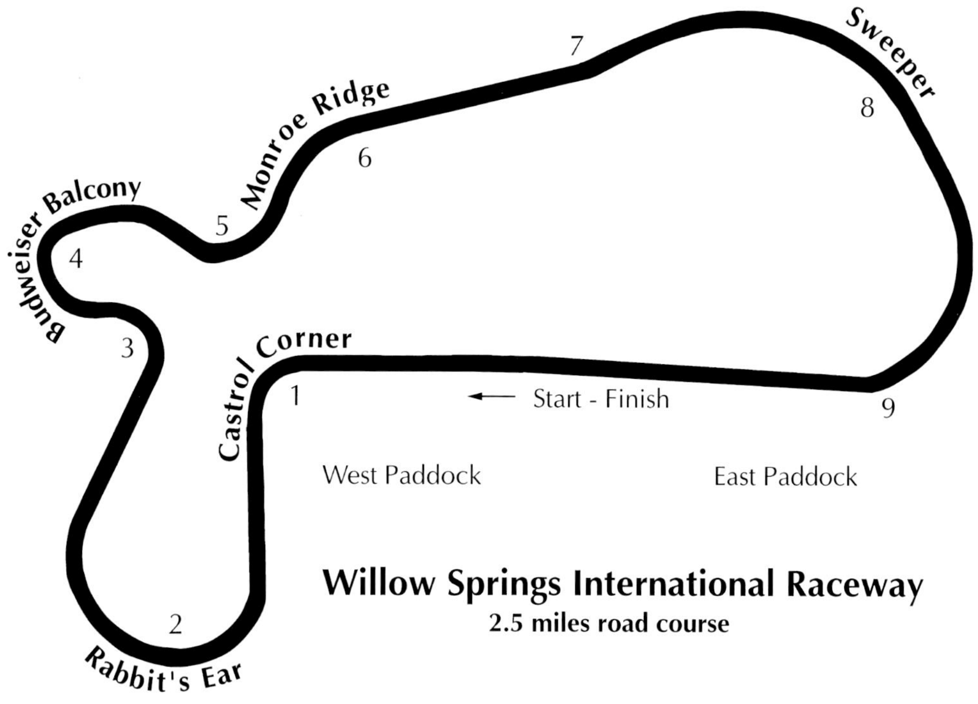

Willow Springs International Raceway
2.5 miles road course

('34 MX4 SS), Alan Moss ('34 MX4 SS), Dale Barry ('34 DTZ Sports) and Red. Dale didn't make it to the starting line because he experienced problems during practice with his newly assembled JAP engine. His engine was making clattering sounds and he didn't want to chance a blow up. His previous engine had blown up a few months earlier when a connecting rod failed while it was idling in his driveway. Dale would return to racing at a later date. The remainder of the group was ready to race. When the pace car pulled off, the race entries were given the green flag.

The quick BMWs burned up the track and five of them finished the race in the top ten spots. A 1939 328S took first, closely followed by a 1933 Alfa Romeo 8C-2300 with another 1938 BMW 328 taking the third spot. Morgan trikes didn't make an appearance until position 18 with Alan Naille's F-Super. Red was right behind him in 19th place. Positions 20 through 22 were filled with a 1925 Duesenberg Indy, 1929 Lagonda and a 1920 Ford Model-T special. Spence Young was next in his 1934 MX4 followed by Alan Moss in his 1934 MX4 SS. The race was run in a time of 22 min. 3.20 sec. for an average of 60.88 mph and a satisfying length of 22.38 miles. Leaders through position 9 all ran 10 laps. All of the Morgan trikes completed 8 laps.

Times posted for Red were primarily in the 2 min. 43-47 sec. range. The fastest time was 2 min. 39.20 sec. during lap 7 when Alan Naille's F-Model was hot on Red's tail. Once his trike got around Red, he wasn't able to make any progress pulling away – Red couldn't gain enough speed coming out of the turns with the 19 tooth sprocket to pass him. A post race observation revealed that the throttle cable on the number 2 carburetor was too short and didn't allow the slide to fully open. That would be corrected for the next event.

Participating in vintage racing at Laguna Seca after an absence since 1984 was marvelous fun. We had no problems with the engine and came away with a great feeling of accomplishment. And then a thought raced through our minds. How fast might Henry Laird have pushed Red at the Laguna Seca Raceway?

One more event was scheduled in 1996: The Willow Springs Porsche-Alfa Challenge V, conducted by VARA on October 12-13 near Rosamond, California. This 2.5 mile course was billed as "The Fastest Track in the West" and it really was – its graceful sweeping turns and long straights offering some fast performance opportunities.

Red was running with the same specifications used for the Laguna Seca meet, still using the 19 tooth sprocket. This ratio was determined to be the best gearing for Willow Springs. The weather was warm with strong afternoon gusty winds that tore at the camp Donna was attempting to keep secured.

Red ran in the practice session for Novices because this was the requirement for VARA participants until they had completed two events and were issued a Competition License. The Saturday practice at 8:30

commenced during cool morning temperatures. The only other Morgan trike entered was the 1934 DTZ Sports driven by Dale Barry. He had corrected the JAP engine problem experienced at Laguna Seca and was looking forward to competing with Red.

The afternoon session was much warmer than the morning one – Red's engine was running hot. On every lap the engine seemed to be tightening, especially while climbing the hill on turns 3 and 4. Red ran better on the straights and was turning times of 2:33.69 to 2:37.54 through four laps. Then disaster struck! The engine began to seize on lap 5 while approaching turn 9 and a signal was given to exit the track. While slowing down and turning left off the track the engine seized solid. The rear wheel locked up and the steering got out of hand. Red veered suddenly and rolled over on its right side, turned upside down, skidded for a short distance and pinned its driver underneath. The race was red flagged and stopped.

The emergency crews and track workers were on the scene immediately and quickly surrounded Red. Donna and the nearby spectators no doubt missed a few heartbeats. As the emergency crew approached, I yelled that I was okay and asked them to lift the trike. The helmet pressing against my chest was making breathing difficult. When Red was righted I was able to scoot out and stand up after they determined I was all right. The crowd cheered when I removed my helmet and waved. My racing suit had a tear in the back just below the neck line and the helmet showed some scuffing. Red and its fortunate driver would race another day.

Red appeared mangled but the damage was not severe. The left side wind scallop was smashed flat against the cowl. The rear view mirror and grab handle had snapped off. Some scuffing marred the paint and numbers on the sides of the body. The fabric cover over the rear wheel was shredded. Both wings were bent and twisted. But that was it – no damage occurred to the wood, chassis, or engine. This was hard to believe until everything had been carefully checked.

Apparently, the action to slow Red when the engine begin to seize, and then folding into the passenger side during the roll, saved us both from disaster. The cage over the rear wheel and the cowling wind scallop substituted as roll bars. Later, a fake roll bar was fabricated from foam pipe insulation and installed as a mock-up to see how Red would look. It was pretty ugly and detracted from Red's historic profile so the idea was shelved.

Over the winter Red got the necessary attention to restore it to racing condition. Both wings were removed and the paint was stripped. Straightening with a body hammer while pounding over a sand bag improved their look prior to repainting. A spare rear view mirror was installed. After searching through many hardware and cabinet shops – even asking British friends to join the hunt – a suitable replacement for the grab handle was located. Donna replaced the scuffed racing numbers with new ones after the paint was touched up. She also fabricated a new rear wheel cover. The old one was preserved for its history.

Red's repairs were carried out from October 15 through December 11, 1996. One vital improvement was to replace both pistons with new ones from Venolia. Tolerances of 9 thousandths at the skirt and 13 at the top of the cylinders were used. John Klein, a machinist friend of Dennis Magri's, honed out the barrels. During the final assembly the main jets in each carburetor were changed to 190 in number one and 240 in number two. On December 17 Red was prepared for its first test drive with the new pistons. The engine sounded good and pulled strongly. Minor adjustments to the clutch and cable systems were required. Red was ready to get back on the track! Overall, even with the accident, 1996 had been a successful racing season.

Surveying the damage sustained at Willow Springs

The idea of organizing a pre-war class of cars for the next meet at Buttonwillow was discussed with Dan Longacre of VARA during the meet at Willow Springs. Dale Barry and I volunteered to work with him to publicize the pre-war class idea. While desiring a good group of early cars, we also wanted to get the largest possible number of Morgan three wheeler entries for the event. Letters, phone calls, and inspiration were funneled into the effort. We had some work to do with the 2nd Annual British Extravaganza scheduled for April 18-20, 1997. As race date approached, it appeared we had 10 entries for a pre-war class – 6 were Morgans and 5 of those were three wheelers. Other three wheeler owners either brought their trikes to support the effort and not race, or came without a trike to participate in the fun.

The prewar cars at Buttonwillow, April 1997

Prewar drivers and supporters. Left to right: Steve Ball, Gary Byrd, Pete Thelander, Larry Ayers, John Benton, Dale Barry, Graham Wallis, George Tollworthy and Walt Kirby

The pre-war entries (listed by year) were: 1922 Ford T Speedster driven by Michael Sharp, Graham and Gilly Wallis' 1929 Lagonda, Donna and I with Red, Gary and Tina Byrd's 1933 Morgan JAP SS, Pete and Fran Thelander's 1934 MG NE, George and Kathy Tollworthy's 1934 JAP SS, Dale and Karen Barry's 1934 DTZ Sports, Butch Bucciarelli's 1935 Wolseley Hornet, Bob Schmidt's 1938 Morgan 4/4 and John and Cynthia Benton's 1949 F4 Morgan. The Morgan three wheelers – and the Flat Rad plus the other British and American cars – got our adrenaline flowing and energized the spectators.

On Friday afternoon most of the Morgan drivers had registered and presented their cars for scrutinizing. The Morgan Clubs of Northern and Southern California hosted a track party for owners, drivers and enthusiasts. Several owners of Morgan four wheelers joined our group to celebrate their participation with four of them competing that weekend.

Saturday dawned a little overcast and cool with enough moisture in the air to produce a brilliant two-minute rainbow over the pits. The damp-air conditions meant the cars would run cooler and probably faster on a track surface which remained dry.

Red drove on to the track at 9 o'clock for a practice session. Drivers had an opportunity to familiarize themselves with the circuit, observe the tightness of the corners, study the line through the turns and determine how their vehicle would handle. After a good practice session, drivers either kicked back or checked over their vehicles.

At noon the officials opened the track for those who wished to do parade laps. The pre-war cars led the official parade lap. All three wheelers, racing or not, were able to experience the track from a driver's viewpoint. A lot of enthusiasm was generated and several trike owners not racing decided they would like to do so in the future.

At 2 PM the pre-war group gathered for their qualifying race. Bob Schmidt's 1938 Morgan 4/4 had problems with a faulty oil pump and brake fading. David Haines and Bob's son, Peter, made adjustments to both which enabled the car to compete for the final event. The 1934 JAP SS driven by George Tollworthy had experienced number one cylinder separation at the flange where it joined the cases while practicing earlier, so he was out. Although he regularly drives his trike and participates in gymkhanas, this was George's first effort at racing. After analyzing the mechanical failure and discussed driving techniques with other drivers, he was determined to return next year.

Red's front carburetor came loose on the first lap and dangled from the front of the engine, held only by the fuel line and control cable. Fortunately, no fuel spilled. The carburetor had been attached with rubber tubing and screw clamps. This mishap proved the carburetors required a more secure method of attachment with a metal flange mounting – not a rubber hose. After returning to the pit, the carburetor was remounted and secured with safety wire. Red received no qualifying time but could race in the final event.

Supercharger woes struck the Wolsley Hornet. The drive failed and knocked it out of the race. John Benton's clutch kept slipping, slowing him way down. The other drivers and vehicles survived the rigors of racing such vintage equipment.

Several special awards – provided by the Morgan Clubs – were presented at the Saturday night BBQ to drivers in the pre-war class. The winners were selected through balloting by popular vote. Favorite three wheeler: Gary Byrd's aluminum bodied 1933 JAP SS. Favorite pre-war racer: Graham Wallis' 1929 Lagonda. The favorite four wheeler Morgan: Bob Schmidt's 1938 4/4. Dan Longacre drew a name from the drivers of pre-war cars for a Racers Choice-Finest Example award furnished by Aardvark International-Talbot & Company. It was a mirror mounted on a wooden plaque and Red was the fortunate recipient. Morgans posting track times received the following recognition. The fastest lap for a three wheeler: Gary Byrd (3:21). The fastest four wheeler Morgan lap: Brian Howlett (2:28).

Seven groups of cars raced throughout the weekend. The pre-war cars were on the track for a warm up exercise at 9 AM on Sunday morning. Hustling to be sure Red was running correctly with its reattached carburetor, some testing was done around the paddock. The number one cylinder was misfiring and traced to a fowled plug which was replaced. Other entrants carried out pre-race checks before the group was summoned to the pre-grid. We drove those little trikes around the circuit as if our lives depended on it and had a ball! The practice session was conducted with out incident and all were ready for the race scheduled for 11:30.

Eight vehicles arrived at the grid for the start and then followed the pace car for one lap before getting the green flag. With the lack of a qualifying time, Red started at the back of the pack. When the green flag dropped its two carbs sucked fuel madly and it shot past the '47 and '38 Morgans before the first turn. There was a delay in catching the others as they were some distance ahead by then. Within a lap and a half Red had passed the '22 Ford T. Dale Barry experienced some two wheel cornering at several locations. The Lagonda diced with the leading trikes – its driver grinning from ear to ear. Byrd 's trike was trying hard to catch the Thelander's MG, but couldn't quite manage it.

The order of finish was: Pete Thelander's '34 MG NE at 3:15.83; second was Gary Byrd's '33 SS at 3:17.00; third, Graham Wallis' '29 Lagonda with 3:18.88; fourth, Larry & Red at 3:23.38; fifth, Dale Barry's '34 DTZ at 3:30.51; sixth was Michael Sharp's '22 Ford at 3:44.55; seventh, Bob Schmidt's '38 4/4 with 3.53.44; and eighth was the '47 F4 driven by John Benton at 4:06.61.

The 5 lap race ran a length of 14.6 miles. It was timed over 16 minutes 33.148 seconds. There were no incidents and everyone finished without anything breaking. As the entrants came in to the pits, each was presented a checkered flag with the VARA insignia. All entrants in the pre-war racing group received flags whether or not they had raced. This nice gesture was a way of thanking those who helped kick off the new VARA class of pre-war cars.

Everyone appreciated Walt and Jane Kirby trailering their newly acquired 1932 JAP Super Aero all the way from Bonners Ferry, Idaho, a distance of 1300 miles each way. Dave Kenny and Robin Yarrow brought Dave's 1936 MX4 barrel back. Steve Ball trailered his 1934 MX Family. All of the MTWC members deserved and were given a huge thanks for their enthusiasm and support. Eight trikes in all for a race meet!

The next race for Red was the 11th Annual Chrysler Wine Country Classic on May 17-18 at Sears Point Raceway. This was a special meet for reasons other than being able to participate with Red. After years of long-distance conversations about Morgans, my father's curiosity led him to make a 1500 mile journey from Texas to join our pit crew and watch the race. Donna and I proudly hosted my 82 year old Dad and his wife, Mary. It was their first visit to a race event at a track location.

Red's pit crew: Donna, at left, flanked by the Ayers clan – Shirle, Mary and Larry

Two other Morgan trikes, the 1934 DTZ Sports driven by Dale Barry, and the 1934 MX4 SS driven by Alan Moss supported the three wheeler effort. The group, comprised of a variety of vehicles, included a 1930 Austin 7, 1936 Riley TT Special, 1952 Jaguar XK-120, 1952 Jowett Jupiter, 1932 Alfa Romeo 8C-2300MM, 1950 MG-TD and a 1958 Crosley Special. There were 35 entries in the class.

The race was 21 miles or 7 laps of the 3 mile circuit. It was run in a time of 15 min. 59.771 sec. with an average of 78.769 mph for the winner, a '56 Cleary Special. This year, there wasn't an official list of times posted, only the order of finishing for the 23 participants. On that list, Red finished in spot 18 followed by a '55 Sunbeam Alpine Tal, Alan Moss' '34 MX4 Morgan and Dale Barry's '34 Morgan DTZ Sports.

Another race successfully completed and three months until the 24th Monterey Historics at Laguna Seca – time to closely check Red and make any adjustments to the engine, chassis, and brakes. There was not much to do other than repair a broken exhaust flange which had cracked. At track side, a temporary patch was made with high temperature silicone but only held for a day. Dick Tuttle later welded the crack and made a new collar for the pipe. Careful checking turned up no other problems. This year, Dick Tuttle and his son, Toby, were asked to be our pit crew. Donna presented them with some red T-shirts for the occasion which displayed the Red Morgan Racing logo.

Saturday morning Red was on the track at 9 AM for practice in group 1A for 1912-1929 Sports Racing Cars. During the session the engine missed a beat or two and Toby Tuttle suggested using a hotter plug. Two new plugs were installed and Red seemed to run better. During the excitement of race day the oil catch can from the crankcase wasn't emptied; this was normally done upon returning to the paddock. Otherwise, we were ready for the race of 10 laps scheduled for 1 PM. Our fellow trike competitor, Dale Barry, was having serious distributor problems and our pit crew assisted with his dilemma. Alan Moss was the only other Morgan trike entry and appeared to be running strong. In fact, if he was really fast in getting away at race start, Red might have trouble catching him. As it developed, he was gridded behind us at the start and Red was able to keep ahead of him.

We were positioned about midway in the field and having fun trying to pass the Ford Model-Ts, but didn't downshift in turn 11 when it might have been advantageous to pass others coming out of that turn. An unusual amount of oil mist appeared on my helmet visor – it was from the oil overflow bottle which wasn't changed after practice – but vision wasn't obstructed. Oil was baking onto the left exhaust pipe. No black flags were raised so things must have been acceptable with the track officials. Onward we went, trying to catch the others. Dale Barry had pulled off the track with continuing distributor malfunctions and Alan Moss wasn't far behind in his trike. Several of the faster Bugattis lapped us, but the bronze JAP engine was running well with the hotter plugs and Red surged onward to complete 9 laps before the race concluded finishing in position 14 behind several Bugattis, a Bentley, Austin 7 and a Stutz. Red recorded a time of 2:44.47 on lap 8 which beat our fastest time in qualifying at 2:44.61 allowing us to finish ahead of a 1923 Essex, a Lagonda, and several model-T Fords, one placing last in 23rd position. With two successful racing seasons now completed, we felt like chasing Laird's record for the number of races entered, although that goal was still some distance away.

Red's first race of 1998 was the 3rd Annual British Extravaganza conducted by VARA and sponsored by Moss Motors on May 1-3 at Buttonwillow Raceway Park. The organizers hoped that a record number of pre-war vehicles for this event would enter, perhaps numbering twenty. The reality – 6 Morgan trikes and 10 other vehicles in the class. Several entries canceled at the last moment. Among those who showed were a '33 Alfa Romeo Monza, a '39 Lagonda V12, '34 MG-NE, '36 Kurtis-Ford, '19 Essex, '15 Saxon and a '34 MG Magnette.

The Morgan trikes entered were the '33 SS driven by Gary Byrd, John Benton's '49 F4, the '34 JAP SS belonging to George Tollworthy, Dale Barry's '34 DTZ Sports, Alan Moss' '34 MX4 SS and Donna and I with Red.

The trikes ran well during practice and everyone was excited about qualifying. However, the weather forecast for the weekend wasn't promising with the effects of *El Niño* still very prominent. Before Saturday qualifying, the skies opened up. Between showers, drivers were asked to take non-racing vehicles onto the track surface to help dry it. During qualifying, the track was still a bit slippery so Red took it easy and only slid its rear wheel on a couple of turns, never losing control or executing evasive maneuvers.

The weather continued wet throughout Saturday night and into Sunday morning. We had a leisurely breakfast and decided to skip practice and not run on the slippery track surface. The organizers chose to modify the schedule and moved our pre-war race up from one o'clock to noon. That felt right and Red seemed eager to get onto the track now that it was drying. The previous day the racer posted the fastest qualifying among the other Morgan trikes and seemed ready to continue its success.

When the pace car pulled off the track there was a roar of twin engines as the green flag fell. The '33 Alfa Monza surged ahead, and was not going to be caught by any of the Morgans. Two groups of Morgans – Gary Byrd, Dale Barry, and Al Moss in the first – George Tollworthy and John Benton further back in a second – were chasing Red. We tried to catch the '29 Lagonda driven by Graham Walls. Pete Thelander, in his '34 MG, was chasing the '52 MG driven by Rob Squire who was chasing the Monza leading the pack.

Red was running strongly and swapped positions with the Lagonda several times before it begin pulling slowly away. With a dry track, everyone was able to let out the throttle and go as fast as they dared.

Mechanical causalities overtook the '19 Essex which quit after 3 laps. The MG Magnette, '48 Lester-MG, '36 Kurtis-Ford, and '39 Lagonda V12 also pulled out. The Morgans placed in positions 5 through 11 in this order – Red in 5th, Byrd's '33 in 6th, Barry's '34 in 7th, the '34 Matchless driven by Moss in 8th – then the '15 Saxon driven by Tom DeMund snuck in the lineup. Tollworthy with his '34 came in 10th followed by Benton's '49 F4. This had been the largest turnout of Morgan trikes on the West Coast for a sanctioned racing event!

Over the fourth of July weekend, a special event took place in Visalia, California to commemorate the revival of the Visalia Road Races of 1912-17. A special invitation

The prewar entries at Buttonwillow, May 1998

was extended to owners of Morgan three wheelers for this 85th Anniversary because the event organizers wanted to spot light three wheelers and pre-war racers. Mooney Grove Park was the site for a variety of autos and motorcycles for driving exhibits and a concours.

The local newspaper, *The Visalia Times-Delta,* ran an article titled, "Mad For Morgans" featuring a photo of four Morgan trikes owned by George Tollworthy, Dale Barry, John Benton and I. A fifth trike owner, Ed Berghino, brought his trike to the event but hadn't been present for the photo.

Spectators gather to see a demonstration of Red's engine starting process

The weekend was a fund raiser for the Boys and Girls Club of Tulare County and the trikers gave rides to lucky kids who had entered a trike coloring contest sponsored by the local paper. The local Fox TV station covered the event, as well as several representatives from magazines and radio stations. They generated a lot of publicity for this good cause, raised money, and the *Men of Trikes* had a great time participating. A nice surprise was a first place award presented to Red in the Morgan Class at the Sunday concours. The trike belonging to George Tollworthy took home a third place award in the concours. The trikes made a good showing. George was also featured in an interview airing on local television covering his impressions of owning and driving a three wheeled vehicle. I participated in a radio interview and spoke about Morgan trikes, obtaining parts, racing and the Morgan Three Wheeler Club. The organizers hoped the Visalia event would become as well known as Hershey.

With both Buttonwillow and Visalia behind us, and the J.A.P. engine running strong, we looked forward to participating in the 25th Monterey Historic Automobile Races in August. This anticipation was made even more special because my sister, Diana Seitz, and her friend, Gregory Bade from Houston, were going to share pit crew duties with Donna and her brother, Dennis Olsen, and his wife Sharon from Colorado Springs. The event this year at Laguna Seca highlighted the great Porsche cars and there were dozens of them in attendance to celebrate their 50th Anniversary.

Red's pre-war class was comprised of four Morgan trikes: the '34 DTZ driven by Dale Barry, a '47 F-Super belonging to Alan Naille, Al Moss' '34 MX4 SS, and Donna and I with Red. Glorious weather prevailed throughout the weekend with dozens of traditional parties, auto auctions, car displays and racing.

Friday morning practice for our group was in the company of a '22 Delage, '23 Bugatti Tank, '27 Bentley, several Ford specials, a '23 Essex and a group of Ford Model-Ts. The Morgans held their own and appeared to be running well, except that Red's power seemed down and wasn't approaching its performance in May at Buttonwillow. Tinkering with the carburetor and plugs didn't improve the situation, so we decided to wait until Saturday morning qualifying and see what developed.

Saturday qualifying resulted in times for Red from 2:51.38 to 3:23.46, with the number one cylinder still down on power. Would Red be able to be competitive or even finish the race in this state? The pit crew assembled to lay good vibrations upon the driver and his mount.

The plugs were changed and carburetors adjusted until it was time to suit up and get out there. During the race some position swaps took place between Dale's '34 DTZ and Red on several laps. The two trikes driven by Moss and Naille were ahead of Red about two blocks when the yellow flag came out after a vehicle (not a Morgan!) lost a wheel and stopped in the middle of the track near turn eleven. There were two laps under full course yellow with no passing, one-fifth of the race! The trikes, however, all completed racing with no mechanical or other problems. No mean feat! Hearty congratulations to the Men of Trikes.

Red's times actually improved to 2:41.74 under full throttle down the main straight and finished in 9th position after starting in the 12 spot. The Morgans proudly finished in places 6 through 11 behind a Delage, Bugatti, Fronty Ford, Austin 7 and Flathead Special. Following the Morgans were 3 Ford Model-Ts, a Duesenberg, a '14 Ford Racer and a '23 Essex. During the weekend Morgan owners from as far away as Australia and Japan visited our paddock area.

Following the event, Red was examined to determine the problem with the number one cylinder, beginning with a compression check. This cylinder would only show 30 while the number two registered 55 – not much better. The engine had to come off the chassis to remove the heads. Once that was done, the valves were pulled. The heads and valve assemblies went to John Klein for advise. He lapped the valves, ground the seats and honed the cylinders. When the engine was reassembled and installed the compression jumped to 100 in the number two cylinder and to 95 in number one. Red was back in business. Nothing else was flagged as a problem area. Red was road tested in anticipation of racing with CSRG in October at Thunder Hill.

The annual All-British Car Meet took place in Palo Alto on September 13, not far from the Stanford Campus. Nearly every make of British automobile was represented with the total number of cars approaching 600. Red was dressed to thrill in "full racing trim" with a roll bar, rear spoiler and front air dam. The roll bar was fabricated from pipe insulation foam while the other components were constructed from foam core. From a distance all of it appeared very real because the items were painted to match the trike.

Red was displayed with 13 other Morgan four wheelers representing the class. The Triumph Club, with 48 entries, took home the award for the largest club participation. Red was the recipient of an engraved pewter mug for the best pre-war entry.

Red's last race event in 1998 was at Thunder Hill Park near Willows, California. Sponsored by CSRG, the oldest racing organization in the West and the second oldest in the U.S., this was their 30th Season Finale. The course, set in rolling foothills, featured fifteen turns over three miles. Turn five was discovered to be a miniaturized version of turn 8-8A, the famed corkscrew at Laguna Seca. Red should have a lot of fun on this track.

Saturday morning began with a practice session accompanied by other pre-war cars. CSRG and various pre-war owners had publicized this event to organize the early cars. An entry of at least 10 pre-war vehicles would assure our own race. We achieved that number by including Dennis Glavis' '53 Morgan, Tom Franges '57 Cooper, and Rob Squire's '52 MG TD in the class.

The pace was set by Peter Gidding's '35 Alfa Romeo 8c who managed to avoid the slower cars while lapping them. Other class entries were: Fred Huttleston's '19 Essex, Gary Lucas' '15 Ford Model-T, Tom DeMund's '15 Saxon, Fred Temp's '20 Rajo Special, Robert Schimdt's '38 Morgan 4/4, George Tollworthy's '34 Morgan JAP SS and our '30 Morgan JAP Super Aero, Red.

During the Saturday morning warm up the starter motor came loose on the Glavis '53 Morgan and Temps' Rajo Special oil line fractured into a valve chamber. Gary Lucas' 1915 Ford T speedster was passengered by his riding mechanic, Bruce Hudkins, who had fun playing the part of a vintage racer.

Red in disguise with modern aero-package

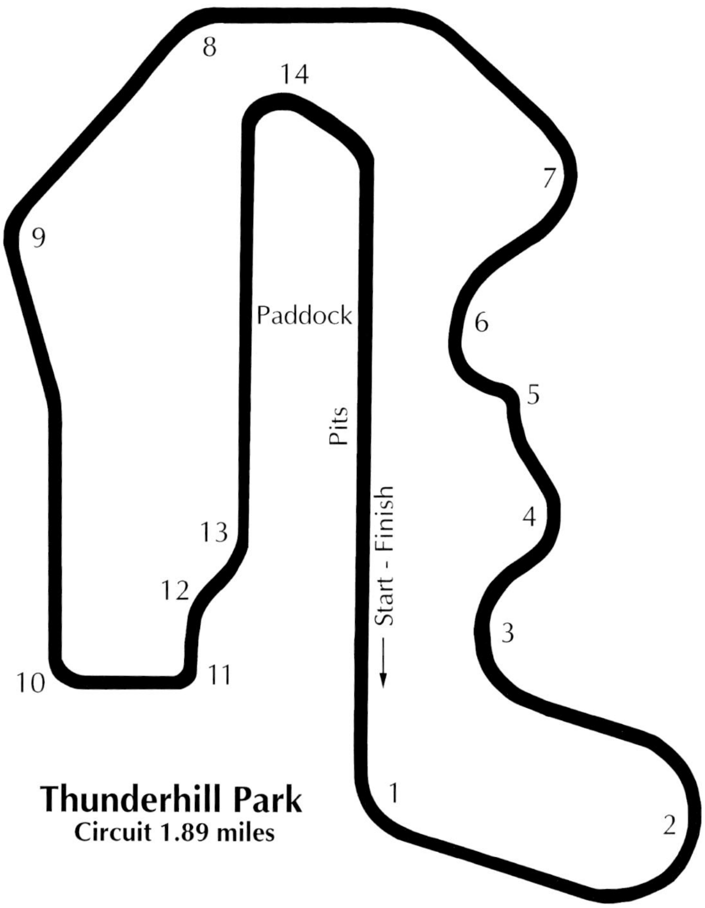

Thunderhill Park
Circuit 1.89 miles

A new event was added to this year's meet – a pursuit race. Cars were given a handicap depending on their age and speed and started by time clock. This proved to be a popular event with a number of entries. We elected to save Red's engine from stress and not participate, but George Tollworthy entered his '34 Morgan and became the oldest vehicle to finish the event. His trike was awarded a silver tray at the awards banquet on Saturday night.

The race Saturday afternoon proved exciting between the Morgan entries and we enjoyed turns passing each other trying to prove who had the fastest entry. Only the very fast '35 Alfa Romeo, the '52 MG TD, and the quick '19 Essex proved faster than the Morgans. Peter Schmidt, driving his dad's beautiful '38 Morgan 4/4, beat Red to the finish line. Red took the checkered ahead of Tollworthy's '34 JAP who lead the Ford T, Saxon and Rajo. There were no mishaps and all the Morgans performed very well. This track was so friendly to our pre-war entries that we promised to return the following year for more racing excitement. Many of the pre-war drivers feel there is growing interest in this early class of vehicle and the various organizations who choose to include a pre-war class in their events will eventually find success with that goal. Red certainly enjoys the sport of racing with the older wheels and we're happy to tag along whenever it goes out for some track adventures.

Driving a Three Wheeler

Many drivers who have never been in a three wheeler make four basic observations. The first is that three wheel cars exhibit unique handling characteristics. Second, they have a tendency to oversteer. Third, they exhibit a tendency to become two wheelers through turns. Fourth, they display the characteristic of turning over. This latter point is not so much an inherent trait of the vehicle as a response to the behavior of the driver.

Drivers generally agree that they prefer a car which understeers – also called push or plow – when a car turns less than it should, rather than the opposite, a car that tends to oversteer – loose or stepping out – when it turns more than it should with a given effort. Apparently, trikes with a single wheel in front will oversteer when they reach their limits of tire adhesion. Therefore, one might think that it preferable to have a reverse tricycle, i.e. a trike with two wheels in front and one at the rear, and deal with understeer.

When driving a Morgan trike, about the only way to get into trouble is when the brakes are locked while turning a corner. The rear of the vehicle then tries to catch with the front which might cause a spin-out or roll-over. The solution is to corner under power, braking before the corner in a straight line, and then bring the trike around under control. When racing, this is usually the fastest way through most turns. Don't use too much power going through a turn when the speed can't be controlled. With too much power pushing against too much steering lock at too slow a speed it's difficult to provoke a break away from either the front or the rear tires. Be ready to reduce power and apply some opposite lock if trouble seems likely. Try to keep things smooth and that extra speed can be utilized when needed.

H.F.S. Morgan judged it right when he produced the first three wheeler having the single driving wheel at the rear. The balance and handling of the trike constantly demonstrates the correctness of this decision. Most modern three wheelers manufactured today have two at the front with few exceptions. The Reliant Robin is an example of the opposite approach.

The oversteer-understeer of a three wheeler results from many characteristics involving suspension, engine placement, tire size type and pressure, steering configuration and roll and weight distribution.

The Morgan, with its chain driven rear wheel, demonstrates good balance and road adhesion, but has its limitations. For example, it will demonstrate a tendency to dance around curves under power unless the rear wheel is dampened with more than the standard leaf springs. A shock absorber on either side of the rear wheel, like those installed on Red, assist in keeping the rear wheel on the surface. It will still bounce if tire pressure is too high. Red runs comfortably with 30-35 pounds in the rear. Others might prefer more pressure, particularly on the four cylinder F-models. Thirty-five pounds in the rear is probably the limit with conventional tires.

The front wheels, using Avon SM MK II tires, give a satisfactory performance with 25 pounds pressure. Driving Red under power around tight corners at turn seven at Sears Point, or turn eleven at Laguna Seca, I experience the sensation of power drifting, as the rear wheel tracks the fronts when I pull out of turns. However, more often than not, the single rear wheel produces squealing. The tire patches, or ground contact points, aren't very wide with narrow motorcycle tires. Trikes racing in England are permitted the use of slicks which improves the situation.

The weight shift while cornering may allow one of the front wheels to become airborne. This is the principal reason that trikes racing in Europe carry passengers. The passenger serves as ballast and aids in keeping the left side wheel down on the track helping to distribute the overall balance of the three wheeler.

Having a low center of gravity is also very useful and one of the strong points for modifying trikes for racing. Widening the track and lowering the body on the frame accomplishes this. Examples of this are found in Europe, Australia and the United States.

Driving a three wheeler is always a lot of fun, especially if it can be put on the track to compete against others of a similar vintage and power. All of them are rare machines – eye catchers – always popular with spectators who love to photograph them and ask questions. The excitement and fun of driving a chain driven three wheeler is unbeatable!

Race Preparing a Morgan

The general intent when participating with sanctioned racing organizations is to share the racing experience, not necessarily to win, but to have fun and exhibit the vehicle's history. There are no awards to be won at most vintage races, but there is certainly a lot to be lost if your vehicle fails and causes an accident, or you cause one due to driver error. So, the first step in preparation for racing is not necessarily how the vehicle is being detailed, but in knowing yourself and why you want to go to the race course.

When serious about preparing a trike for the track, there are certain helpful guidelines. Safety is strongly stressed with organizations which sanction vintage races. Throughout the U.S. these organizations require similar safety equipment compliance before competing in their events.

It is always a good idea to get a copy of that respective organization's rule book before proceeding. Most organizations encourage the restoration, preservation and use of historic sports and racing cars. They emphasize the importance of retaining the correct configuration of the body, engine and chassis. Modifications which were not available at the time of original manufacture or made during historical racing campaigns are frowned upon. Over restoration falls under the same criterion. The goal is to restore the trike to the condition which the manufacturers would realize, if they were doing the work.

As far as the physical preparation of the trike, there are certain guidelines and regulations to be followed which will almost certainly assure passing tech inspection, mandatory before each race.

Those who have converted their trikes from mechanical to hydraulic brakes will not be penalized for not adhering to authenticity. If mechanical brakes are preferred, invest in some composition bonded linings which work better the hotter they become to avoid brake fade. At least one operational brake light must be used. There are restrictions on the make of tire and each organization has guidelines. Tire sizes should follow those furnished by the Morgan Factory or as close as possible. No slicks. Some Morgan racing drivers prefer the Avon SM MK II tires with their zig-zag tread pattern. Close inspection should reveal no loose or broken wheel spokes.

All drain plugs, axle and steering retaining nuts, and gearbox mounting nuts or bolts should be safety wired. Safety wiring consists of drilling through the nut corners or through bolts and wiring them to the frame or some other permanent part which will prevent the fastener from coming off if it loosens. Safety wire and special pliers for twisting wire are available through many hardware stores and tool supply houses. All steering and suspension parts should always be secured with safety nuts and cotter pins.

Catch cans of at least one quart capacity must be used for the radiator and crankcase, especially on total loss oiling systems. Water, not glycol-based coolant, is required. The latter is slippery and difficult to remove from the track surface.

Everything about the car should be tidy and secure. If there is any doubt about anything, correct it before attempting to pass tech inspection. There is a lot of common sense involved in having your machine clean and presentable. Emphasis is placed on minimal steering play, the installation of neat wiring, and everything properly secured in the correct manner.

Headlight lenses need to be taped. A master ignition cut-off switch, mounted outside the car and clearly marked, is strongly recommended, but not required. Most owners choose to avoid this modification to the outside of their trike for the sake of appearance. The hot terminal side of the battery must be insulated to prevent grounding and the battery must be securely mounted and have leak proof caps. A mirror that provides an adequate rear view is required. Two fender mounted mirrors in addition would provide better views.

There must be no fuel or oil leaks. A clearly marked fuel shut off might be installed, although it isn't required by HMSA, CSRG or VARA. Since trikes have threaded screw-on fuel and oil caps, there is no requirement to use wired-on caps.

A lap seat belt must be used which is at least three (3) inches in width with a metal-to-metal quick release buckle. It should be firmly attached to the metal frame. One way to accomplish this is to employ steel braided cable and cable securing hardware and run the cable through the metal end hole of the seat belt and around a chassis cross member. Or, drill through the wood and use large eye bolts and washers. Explore both.

A fire extinguisher of at least 2.5 pounds capacity, nontoxic, commercially available, should be easily accessible in the cockpit. If more safety is desired, install an onboard fire suppression system, not required, although recommended by VARA.

Race preparing a Morgan three wheeler shares many of the same methods and safety requirements specified for other vehicles, with several differences. The exceptions are that a roll bar, shoulder harness, fuel cell and fire suppression system aren't required on a Morgan trike. These two latter items may be a good idea, however, since safety is a priority.

Event organizers realize that motorsport competition contains a certain amount of risk and that is the reasoning behind the clothing requirements. All clothing items are safety oriented for your protection and that of your fellow competitors.

Helmets must display a Snell Foundation safety sticker date of SA-90 or later. Helmets must be intended for automotive use. Motorcycle helmets will not be accepted, even if your trike is registered as a motorcycle! Only the SA designation is acceptable! The SA-90 helmet date may soon be updated. Get the latest year and helmet you can buy and be safe. A full face shield must be worn in open cars (like Morgans) and have non-breakable glasses. A full face helmet provides the best coverage and protection.

Drivers must wear a clean, one-piece racing type driver suit made of Nomex, PBI or equivalent fire resistant material. If the suit is not constructed of two or more layers of fire protective material, suitable fire protective underwear, including socks, must be worn. Fire resistant underwear is not required with suits of 3 or more layers. Gloves of fire resistant materials (Nomex) or leather with no holes must be used. Shoes must be of fire resistant material or leather on top and at least ankle high. Racing shoes are recommended.

When entering an event, drivers indicate a choice of vehicle identification numbers. These numbers must be 2-3 inches in width by 14-15 inches high and displayed on each side of the trike. They should be a contrasting color to the body to be easily read. Sticky vinyl or contact paper works well for making your own numbers.

If the vehicle doesn't have a log book, one will be issued at tech inspection. A medical card, renewable every two years, must be obtained through a form available from either HMSA, CSRG, VARA and others. Most use identical forms. This form is filled out by the driver and his physician during the physical. The medical card and vehicle log book are required for all drivers entering speed events.

The HMSA organization (Monterey Historics and others) lists Morgan three wheelers as Group 1-A, Sports and Racing Cars. The VARA organization categorizes three wheel Morgans as Historic pre-war vehicles as does CSRG.

I hope this information is useful for those considering competitive events with their pre-war Morgan or other vintage vehicle. Please contact the organizations and request their rule books, medical forms and membership applications.

Epilogue

The intent of this book has been to research and record the complete history of Red and its accomplishments to date. If readers feel this goal has been achieved, and have enjoyed reading about the episodes herein, this project has certainly been worth the fun and effort.

Over the past several racing seasons we've enjoyed tremendous fun sharing Red and the racing experience with others. We've met really nice people who share a common love for their cars in displaying and racing them.

I believe Red will continue to hold the interest of friends, supporters and Morgan enthusiasts. It has been, and hopefully, will continue to be an exciting experience to campaign this historic Morgan three wheel racer.

Appendices

Appendix I
Specifications

1930 Morgan Super Aero
Manufactured by The Morgan Motor Co. Ltd.
Pickersleigh Road, Malvern Link
Worcestershire, England

Engine	JAP JTOR wet sump 50-degree air cooled twin
Displacement	1084 cc
Horsepower	approx. 55 @ 4500 rpm
Bore/Stroke	80 X 107 mm
C.R.	6.5:1
Valves	OHV – 2 per cylinder
Cams	4 – gear driven to enclosed push rods
Cases	Aluminum-bronze (special)
Cylinders	Cast iron finned
Heads	Baronia bronze (special) dog-ear rocker supports
Fuel	4 gal capacity, gravity flow
Oil	1 gal capacity, Pilgrim gear driven double pump
Carburetion	2 Amal 30 mm concentrics
Ignition	Lucas magneto
Electrics	12 volts – starter, stop light, horn (no lights)
Body	Wooden body frame, steel panels
Chassis	Tubular steel, soldered lug construction

Dimensions

Length	118"
Width O.A.	60"
Wheelbase	87"
Track	58"
Height	36"
Grnd Clearance	4-$^{1}/_{2}$"
Weight	975 lb.

Brakes

Front	8" vented drum – Bowden cable
Rear	8" mechanical drum – Bowden cable

Wheels

Front	29 x 3" wire spoke
Rear	29 x 4" wire spoke

Tires

Front	Avon SM MK II 350 x 19
Rear	Avon SM 65S 400 x 19

Suspension

Front	sliding pillars, Newton oil shocks
Rear	pivoting forks, $^{1}/_{4}$ elliptical springs, Hartford friction shocks
Steering	Reduction box 2:1 ratio, $^{3}/_{4}$ turn lock to lock

Gearbox

Trans.	Manual "D" gearbox with sprocket
Gears	3 speeds forward and reverse
Final Drive	Drum sprocket 38 teeth Reynolds chain .75" x 58.5" x 78 links

Instruments
Best & Lloyd mechanical hand pump (for No. 2 cylinder)
Pressure gauge (for supercharger, when fitted) 0-6 psi
Speedometer 0-105 mph
Tachometer 0-8,000
Magneto *kill* switch
Smith's time clock
St. Christopher's mascot

Controls
Levers on steering wheel – throttle, choke, magneto
Gear shift lever on torque tube
Clutch & brake pedals (for rear wheel)
Hand lever for front brake
Hand brake for parking
Engine compression release lever inside cockpit

Accomodations
Seating capacity – two, side by side

Head Room	Unlimited
Seat Width	11"
Seat Travel	Fixed
Leg Room	39"
Knee Room	Little

Road Test Best Results

SS Mile	81.568 mph (1935)
SS Kilo	72.288 mph (1935)
Top	103 mph (1936)

Appendix II
Red's Racing Campaigns

16 Aug 1930	BROOKLANDS. BMCRC (Brooklands Motor Cycle Racing Club), Arthur Maskell, driver.
Apr 1933	DONINGTON PARK. Whitsun, Passenger Machine Event. Henry Laird, driver. Richard Laird, passenger.
22 Jul 1933	BROOKLANDS. LCC (Light Car club) Relay Races. Morgan Factory Team No. 5 Henry Laird, driver. Richard Laird, passenger.
7 Aug 1933	DONINGTON PARK. Bank Holiday. Henry Laird, driver.
9 Sep 1933	BROOKLANDS. MCC Meeting. Henry Laird, driver.
2 Apr 1934	DONINGTON PARK. Sidecar and 3 wheeler event. Henry Laird, driver. Richard Laird, passenger.
20 May 1934	DONINGTON PARK. Whitsun, 10 lap race. Henry Laird, driver. Richard Laird, passenger.
21 Jul 1934	BROOKLANDS. LCC Relay Races. Morgan Factory Team No. 4. Henry Laird, driver. Richard Laird, passenger.
6 Aug 1934	DONINGTON PARK. Bank Holiday. Henry Laird, driver. Richard Laird, passenger.
22 Apr 1935	DONINGTON PARK. 10 Lap Passenger Race for 3 Wheelers and Motorcycle Combinations. Henry Laird, driver. Richard Laird, passenger.
18 May 1935	DONINGTON PARK. Grand Prix 10 Lap Passenger Race. Henry Laird, driver. Richard Laird, passenger.
25 May 1935	BROOKLANDS. BMCRC Cup Day. Henry Laird, driver. Richard Laird, passenger.
10 Jun 1935	BROOKLANDS. 25 Mile Passenger Handicap Race. Henry Laird, driver. Richard Laird, passenger.
26 Jun 1935	BROOKLANDS. BMCRC meet. Henry Laird, driver. Bill Clarke, passenger.
20 Jul 1935	BROOKLANDS. LCC Relay Races. Morgan Factory Team No. 3. Henry Laird, driver. Richard Laird, passenger.
5 Aug 1935	DONINGTON PARK. Bank Holiday. Henry Laird, driver. Richard Laird, passenger.
22 Oct 1935	BROOKLANDS. World Record Attempts for SS Mile and Kilometer. Henry Laird, driver.
23 Oct 1935	BROOKLANDS. BMCRC 5 Lap Mountain Handicap. Henry Laird, driver. Tom Bryant, passenger.
13 Apr 1936	DONINGTON PARK. 10 Lap Sidecar Handicap Event. Henry Laird, driver. Richard Laird, passenger.
May 1936	BROOKLANDS. Race Meet. Henry Laird, driver. Richard Laird, passenger.
1 Jun 1936	DONINGTON PARK. Whit Monday 25 Mile Passenger Race. Henry Laird, driver. Richard Laird, passenger.
3 Aug 1936	DONINGTON PARK. Bank Holiday. Henry Laird, driver. Richard Laird, passenger.
4 Aug 1936	DONINGTON PARK. 25 Mile Passenger Handicap Event. Henry Laird, driver. Richard Laird, passenger.
10 Oct 1936	BROOKLANDS. BMCRC Hutchinson 100. Henry Laird, driver. Richard Laird, passenger.
29 Mar 1937	DONINGTON PARK. Easter Monday. Henry Laird, driver. Michael Faraday, passenger.
17 May 1937	DONINGTON PARK. Whitsun Monday. Henry Laird, driver. Michael Faraday, passenger.
2 Aug 1937	DONINGTON PARK. Bank Holiday. Henry Laird, driver. Rodney Bainbridge, passenger.
11 Sep 1937	BROOKLANDS. Hutchinson 100 Handicap Race. Henry Laird, driver. Bill Clarke, passenger.
27 May 1939	DONINGTON PARK. 8 Lap Sidecar Race. Tom Bryant, driver.
5 Aug 1939	DONINGTON PARK. Sidecar Race. Tom Bryant, driver.
3 Sep 1949	BLANDFORD ARMY CAMP. Sidecar Race. Tom Bryant, driver.
29 Apr 1950	BLANDFORD ARMY CAMP. ACU (Auto Cycle Union) International Race. Tom Bryant, driver.
6 Aug 1951	THRUXTON AERODROME. ACU International Road Race. Tom Bryant, driver.
20 May 1984	LAGUNA SECA. HMSA (Historic Motor Sports Association) Special Event. Larry Ayers, driver.
7-9 Jun 1996	SEARS POINT RACEWAY. HMSA 10th Annual Mollie Stone's Wine Country Classic. Larry Ayers, driver.
14-16 Jun 1996	BUTTONWILLOW RACEWAY. VARA (Vintage Auto Racing Association) Inaugural British Extravaganza. Larry Ayers, driver.
15-18 Aug 1996	LAGUNA SECA. HMSA 23rd Monterey Historic Automobile Races. Larry Ayers, driver.

12-13 Oct 1996	WILLOW SPRINGS INTERNATIONAL RACEWAY. VARA Meet. Larry Ayers, driver.
18-20 Apr 1997	BUTTONWILLOW RACEWAY PARK. VARA 2nd. Annual British Extravaganza. Larry Ayers, driver.
16-18 May 1997	SEARS POINT RACEWAY. HMSA 11th Annual Chrysler Wine Country Classic. Larry Ayers, driver.
14-17 Aug 1997	LAGUNA SECA. HMSA 24th Monterey Historic Automobile Races. Larry Ayers, driver
1-3 May 1998	BUTTONWILLOW RACEWAY PARK. VARA 3rd Annual Buttonwillow Extravaganza. Larry Ayers, driver.
13-16 Aug 1998	LAGUNA SECA. HMSA 25th. Monterey Historic Automobile Races. Larry Ayers, driver.
16-18 Oct 1998	THUNDER HILL. CSRG 30th Season Finale. Larry Ayers, driver.
19-21 Mar 1999	SEARS POINT RACEWAY. CSRG 31st Season Opener. Larry Ayers, driver.
1-2 May 1999	BUTTONWILLOW RACEWAY PARK. VARA 4th Annual Buttonwillow Extravaganza. Larry Ayers, driver.
11-12 Sep 1999	SEARS POINT RACEWAY. CSRG "Yankee Doodle Dandy." Larry Ayers, driver.
15-17 Oct 1999	THUNDER HILL. CSRG 31st Season Finale. Larry Ayers, driver.

Appendix III
Morgan Factory and Racing Milestones

1909 Morgan prototype built with tiller steering.
1910 First Morgan Standard production model single seater. Tiller steering, two chains, no front brakes. External band brake on rear.
1911 First production Two Seater with steering wheel – JAP 964 cc motor.
1912 Morgan Motor Co. Ltd. founded by H.F.S. Morgan. Prototype four seater built.
First Morgan raced at Brooklands – BMCRC International Cyclecar Scratch race.
1913 W.G. McMinnies & Frank Thomas won The Grand Prix Cyclecar Race.
1914 Munitions produced at Morgan Factory during World War I.
G.F. Allen raced Morgan trike at Combination Park, Medford, Massachusetts.
1919 Petrol rationing ended – motor sports competition resumed.
French Morgan production arranged under Morgan Factory license.
1920 Pickersleigh Road Works had 160 workers - produced 30 trikes weekly.
Detachable rear wheels – standard length chains.
1921 Standard Poplar model at 50 Pounds Sterling – 50 mph and 60 mpg – electrical lighting optional.
1923 Front brakes became optional at extra cost. Disc wheel covers.
1924 Standard Model with JAP or Blackburne motor for 110 Pounds – electrical starter at additional cost. Aero Blackburne model – 70 mph and 35 bhp. E.B. Ware and T.R. Allchin crashed during JCC at Brooklands – three wheelers banned from racing.
1925 JAP ohv water-cooled 50-deg motor. Electric lights became standard. Harold Beart had fastest unsupercharged 1100 cc car in the world for one way flying start mile at 97.32 mph.
1926 Last Grand Prix model – Anzani motor. Front wheel brakes cost extra. JAP LTOW motor introduced. Britain's Great General Strike affected motoring.
1927 Factory produced 1700 Morgans – peak year! Front 7" brakes standard. LTOWC 10/40 JAP SS Aero, 80 mph. Chassis lowered 2.5", underslung rear springs, knockout rear wheel spindle, Hartford shocks on front.
1928 D-cutouts replaced louvers on cowl of Super Aeros. Van delivery model. Front wheel brakes standard.
1929 M-chassis with detachable bevel box – forged steel underslung rear forks.
1930 New Cyclecar Club becomes Light Car Club. Gwenda Stewart reached 113.52 mph – 5 kilometer record – fastest speed ever for three wheeled cyclecar. Clive Lones and Robin Jackson awarded Brooklands Gold Stars.
1931 C-chassis – two piece propshaft, center bearing. Reverse "R" gearbox, detachable wheels, cycle type wings.
1932 JAP 60-deg ohv wc LTOWZ motor with coil ignition. Detachable, interchangeable wheels standard. Cone clutch replaced by dry plate type. Wings with center rib after July 9
1933 Matchless MX motor. F4 Ford four seater with 8 hp 933 cc motor - 70 mph and 40 mpg. Spare wheel on SS mounted in halo position. Two 'D' cutouts in cowl. Matchless MX4 with barrel back body. B&B single plate clutch.
1934 Motors now all Matchless or Ford, JAP optional. Tom Rhodes awarded Gold Star at Brooklands. Morgan Three Wheeler Club formed April 25 at Hendon, disbanded at outbreak of World War II.
1935 JAP motor no longer offered. Spare wheel halo changed to cork-in-bottle on barrel back models. Ford F2 with 8" brakes.
1936 Reverend P.H.G. Morgan died November 10 at age 84. First year of four wheeler 4/4 production. Henry Laird awarded Brooklands Gold Star.
1937 Family model production ceased. Girling brakes in September.
1938 F-Super – 10 hp Ford E93A, 1172 cc – 72 mph.
1939 Matchless MX2 dropped in June. E.B. Ware died May 16 at age 54. Brooklands Race Track closed ending racing there forever. Last motorcycle race at Donington Park for many years.
1940 Morgan Factory produced munitions for World War II – repair and spares deparıments stayed open. No three wheeler production.
1945 Morgan Factory announced Post War models – no twins, only Ford models. Morgan Three Wheeler Club inaugural General Meeting held September 23.

1946 Peter Morgan joined Morgan Factory firm. Final year of Morgan three wheeler production for V-twins.
1947 Nine of last 12 Morgan production twins dispatched to Australia.
1952 Last 20 F-Models left Morgan Factory July 29 ending three wheeler production.
1953 Some F-Models assembled by enthusiasts from parts stock.
1959 H.F.S. Morgan died June 15 at age 77.
1962 Victory at Le Mans 24 hour in 2-liter class with a Plus 4 driven by Christopher Lawrence and Richard Shepherd-Barron on June 23-4. 2,261 miles at an average of 94 mph.
1970 The Morgan Motor Company, Ltd. celebrated 60th Anniversary. Morgan Three Wheeler Club celebrated 25th Anniversary.
1977 Donington Park reopened May 15 for National Motorcycle Race featuring Morgan three wheelers.
1980 Morgan Factory and enthusiasts celebrated 70 years of Morgan production.
1983 Charles Morgan joined Morgan firm as Production Manager.
1984 75 Years of Morgans celebrated worldwide.
1986 Golden Jubilee celebrated – 50 years of four wheeler production.
1991 Morgan Sports Car Club (Morgan 4/4) celebrated 40th Anniversary.
1995 Morgan Three Wheeler Club celebrated 50th Anniversary – 200 trikes assembled in Great Malvern.
1999 The 90th Anniversary of the first Morgan model.

Appendix IV
Red's Owners

5 August 1930	Arthur Maskell, Maskell for Morgans
2 November 1932	John Elford Russel Palmer
15 May 1933	Henry Laird
Early 1939	Tom Bryant, Huxhams Ltd.
March 1955	Hugh Dyer
September 1961	John Staveley and George Oliver at Mercury Motors
October 1961	Paul S. Moyer
15 June 1967	Vic Hyde
4 June 1977	Larry W. Ayers
22 January 1990	Bob Thredder
13 June 1995	Larry W. Ayers

Appendix V
J.A.P. History

The letters JAP are the initials of a British engineer by the name of John Alfred Prestwich born on September 1, 1874 in the Borough of Kensington, London, England. Early in his schooling, he demonstrated an aptitude toward mechanics, mathematics and drafting. At the age of 14, he built a miniature operating stationary steam engine. At age 20, he formed the Prestwich Manufacturing Company at 1 Lansdowne Road, Tottenham. Before he became serious about building motors for motorcycles and other uses, he developed a film projector for the expanding motion picture business. This projector, incorporating two lenses and two shutters, removed the flicker from motion pictures.

After staying in the picture business for 10 years, he built his first single cylinder JAP motor in 1901. The Triumph Cycle Co. Ltd. of Coventry was the first motorcycle manufacturer to use his JAP motor. That beginning mushroomed into something amazing in those early days of this century and soon one of every eight motorcycles made was fitted with a motor manufactured by JAP.

Not content to remain on the ground, a JAP-built airplane with a 40 hp 8 cylinder engine of JAP design flew on April 10, 1910. Even earlier, the air pioneer A.V. Roe used a 6 hp V-twin JAP to power one of his early biplanes. The first airplane to fly mail in Australia was powered by a JAP engine. But the JAP firm was not destined to remain in the flying business, and moved into manufacturing their own motorcycles, cars, spark plugs, carburetors, fluid measuring gauges, industrial motors and even pencils.

The first V-Twin engine was made in 1904. It was developed over the years, as was the single cylinder engine, and its use in countless motorcycles and Morgans accounted for numerous records in racing. Personalities such as Al Page (Chief Designer), Bert LeVack (Development Engineer), E.C.E. Baragwanath and Stanley M. Greening (Technical Advisor) took the JAP firm to the top level of prestige with racing successes.

By 1913, the company was offering 15 different types of motors ranging from a 2.5 hp single to an 8 hp twin. Both Harry Martin and H.F.S. Morgan relied on the dependable JAP engine to achieve their early records at Brooklands. E.B. Ware, Les Bolton (Flying Wedge & Specials), Sterling Moss (996 cc Cooper-JAP) and of course, Henry Laird, Clive Lones and Tom Rhodes owed their successes in part to the JAP firm and their outstanding V-Twin motors.

The Prestwich Manufacturing Company moved to new premises in Northumberland Park in 1911, less than a mile from their present location. The firm became known as J.A. Prestwich and Company, Ltd. in 1918. The business continued there until the company finally closed in 1963. John Alfred Prestwich passed away in 1954. The legacy he left behind with his wonderful JAP motors is enjoyed to the present day. Drivers like Henry Laird would have taken their racing careers in different directions were it not for the JAP engine.

Appendix VI
Membership and Racing Organisations

The Morgan Three Wheeler Club
Eddie Eyes, Membership Secretary
280 Commonwealth Way, Abbey Wood
London SE2 0LD, United Kingdom

The USA Group of the MTWC
Chris Towner, Organizer
56 Brick Hill Road
Orleans, MA 02653

The Morgan Vintage Racers Register
Henry C. Giffin III, Registrar
503 Breezy Point Drive
Norfolk, VA 23511-3909

The Brooklands Society Ltd.
Tony Hutchings, Archivist
38 Windmill Way
Reigate Way, Surrey
England RH2 0JA

Classic Sports Racing Group (CSRG)
P.O. Box 825
Danville, CA 94526
(925) 736-2823

Historic Motor Sports Association (HMSA)
P.O. Box 489
Buellton, CA 93427
(805) 686-9292
FAX (805) 686-9242

Historic Sportscar Racing, Ltd.
3005 Peacock Lane
Tampa, FL 33618
(888) 477-5999, (813) 931-5642 fax (813) 935-9564

Pittsburg Vintage GP Association
1534 Old Coach Road
Newark, DE 19711
(302) 454-719

Pre-war Racing Group
Graham Wallis
2619 Via Pacheco
Palos Verdes Estates, CA 90274
(310) 544-2445

Rocky Mountain Vintage Racing Club (RMVR)
P.O. Box 2096
Estes Park, CO 80517
(970) 586-4500

Society of Vintage Racing Enthusiasts (SOVREN)
4465 West Mercer Way
Merced Island, WA 98040
(206) 232-4644 fax (206) 232-3844

Sportscar Vintage Racing Association (SVRA)
1 Maple Street
Hanover, NH 03755
(603) 640-6161

Sports Car Club of America (SCCA)
9033 E. Easter Place
Englewood, CO 80111
(303) 694-7222

Vintage Auto Racing Association (VARA)
2029 Verdugo Blvd. #1010
Montrose, CA 91020
(800) 280-8272 fax (818) 249-7428

Vintage Auto Racing Assoc. of Canada (VARAC)
87 Troy Street
Mississauga, ON L5G 1S6
(905) 274-8754

Vintage Sports Car Club of America (VSCCA)
170 Wetherhill Road
Garden City, NY 11530

Vintage Sports Car Drivers Association (VSCDA)
3160 Thornapple River Drive
Grand Rapids, MI 49546
(616) 949-8281 fax (616) 949-8281

Bibliography

Title	Author	Publisher
The Story of Brooklands	W. Boddy	Grenville Publishing
Brooklands, The Future?	Wall, Harris, & Nockolds	Brooklands Society
Brooklands Automobile Racing Club	Lord Montagu	The Car Illustrated
Brooklands	P.J. Wallace	Ballantine Books
The Motor Sport Book of Donington	W. Boddy	Grenville Publishing
JAP, The Vintage Years	Jeff Clew	Haynes Publishing Group
JAP, The End of An Era	Jeff Clew	Haynes Publishing Group
Morgan Sweeps the Board	Dr. J.D. Alderson & D.M. Rushston	Gentry Books Ltd.

Periodical	Article	Author - Date
The Bulletin	Various Issues	The Morgan Three Wheeler Club
The Light Car	Various Issues	1935-1938
The Light Car & Cyclecar	Various Issues	1933
Daily Telegraph	Worst Motor Trial on Record	1 Jan 1934
Derby Evening Telegraph	Various Issues	20 May 1935
The Light Car	The Fifth Relay Race	19 April 1935
Das Motorrad		28 Sept. 1935
Motorcycle Sport	The Greatest Morgan Driver	June 1967
Motor Cycling	Various Issues	1933-1950
Motor Cycling	Morgans for Motorists	Henry Laird - 6 June 1940
Motor Cycling	Three-Wheelers and the Sport	5 Nov 1942
Motor Cycling	Donington Days!	Rob Buxton - 6 Feb 1950
Motorcycle Sport	Nostalgia on three wheels	Titch Allen - Dec 1974
Motorcycle Sport	Memories of Morgan days	Leonard Golding - Feb 1975
Motorcycle Sport	Why Mog Men revere Yellow	Titch Allen - Sep 1983
The Classic Motor Cycle	A Mog Called Yellow	Titch Allen - Dec 1987
The Classic Motor Cycle	A Mog Called Red	Larry Ayers - Aug 1988
The Automobile	When Johnny Came Driving Home Again	Malcolm Jeal - Aug 1990